Living
A Grace-Centred
LIFE

Living A Grace-Centred Life

Copyright © 2017 Sam Uhunoma. All Rights Reserved.

No rights claimed for public domain material, all rights reserved. No parts of this publication may be reproduced, stored in any retrieval system, or transmitted in any form or by any means, electronic, mechanical, recording, or otherwise, without the prior written permission of the author. Violations may be subject to civil or criminal penalties.

Unless stated otherwise, all Scriptures are taken from the King James Version of the Holy Bible.

ISBN: 978-1-63308-265-6 (paperback)
       978-1-63308-266-3 (ebook)

Cover and Interior Design by R'tor John D. Maghuyop

1028 S Bishop Avenue, Dept. 178
Rolla, MO 65401

Printed in the United Kingdom

SAM UHUNOMA

Living A Grace-Centred LIFE

Exploring the Content of Grace for Profitable Living

CHALFANT ECKERT
PUBLISHING

ACKNOWLEDGEMENTS

First and foremost, I would like to express my profound gratitude to God Almighty for divine wisdom, revelation, knowledge, understanding and inspiration to write this book.

Also, I want to say a big thank you to my family: my parents, siblings and relatives for their support and words of encouragement towards actualising my dreams.

I have grown spiritually over time because of the places that God exposed me to in order to position me for spiritual growth. So, I will not fail to mention these wonderful churches: *House of the King (Royal House International Ministries)* in Nigeria, *Mountain of Fire* (Nigeria), *Heaven's Intervention Fire Ministries* (Nigeria), *Winners Chapel* (Nigeria) and *Winners Chapel International,* Manchester. I also want to thank the wonderful friends I met in *Winners Chapel International,* Manchester, who encouraged me.

Thanks to all my mentors: May God bless you all.

TABLE OF CONTENTS

INTRODUCTION 9

Chapter 1:	FINDING GRACE 15
Chapter 2:	MIXING FAITH WITH THE WORD OF GRACE 29
Chapter 3:	PUTTING GRACE TO WORK 47
Chapter 4:	RENEWING YOUR MIND WITH THE WORD OF GRACE 57
Chapter 5:	THE UNMERITED FAVOUR DIMENSION OF GRACE 71
Chapter 6:	THE LOVE DIMENSION OF GRACE 89
Chapter 7:	WE ARE ALREADY BLESSED BY GRACE 109
Chapter 8:	REIGNING IN LIFE BY ABUNDANCE OF GRACE 123
Chapter 9:	BE STRONG IN GRACE 145

ABOUT THE AUTHOR 157
ABOUT THE BOOK 158

INTRODUCTION

Living a grace-centred life is possible for every born-again child of God. Jesus lived a grace-centred life and He has enabled us to do likewise. Jesus did not come to live a life that is impossible for us to emulate. He came to teach us *how* to live life. Jesus' life example is our possibility on earth. He is our standard for living. He is the first begotten of a new race, which is the Grace race. He showed us His pattern of living and how to live. He was *grace personified*. As He is so are we in this world (I John 4:17). We are all products of His grace. We must express grace and grow in every facet of it as depicted by Jesus Christ.

Grace has been misinterpreted. The concept has been lost to some misconceptions. Some people religiously say, "I will do it by the grace of God," or "by God's grace, I will achieve" this or that without knowing the actual content of grace. If you say you can do something by the grace of God, you are only applying one aspect of grace which is the aspect of God's enabling power at work in you.

Sometimes people casually name their children "Grace" without realising the power of the name. It's important for us to know what it's all about so that we can make the most out of it. It's time to be conscious of what grace is and apply it to our lives for profitable living.

In my first book, *The Winning Grace, How I Won and Am Still Winning*, (2016, Chalfant Eckert Publishing), I developed a clear definition and an in-depth understanding of grace. Let's explore more on the content of grace for profitable living. The lid has been taken off; we can see more of the content of God's grace. Grace has been uncovered for us to maximise it in our lives. It's not just unmerited favour as we have been taught. It's a huge package God has given unto us to live lives of exploits on earth. Unmerited favour is only one aspect of grace. It's far more than that. The unmerited favour dimension of grace will be discussed in this book as we go along. There is much to grace than we have known. An acronym to help understand the foundation of grace is:

> ***God's***
> ***Reliable***
> ***Abundance by***
> ***Christ's***
> ***Effort***

It's not what you work for, it was all Christ' effort to bring you to a place of rest. You can't afford to settle for less when all things have been done for you by grace. All you need is to respond by faith in His finished work in order to enjoy a life of profit.

Your faith is your now-reality in the finished work of Christ. You are meant to rest by faith in what has been done already. Your faith is the receiver of what grace has transmitted. Every challenge has been handled by grace if you start enforcing your victory by faith. Do something with the grace you have been given. It's your responsibility to make grace count in your life through faith. Put the grace of God to work in your life. Don't wait for God to ask you what you did with the grace He gave to you.

We have been very excited by the message of grace, but now it's time to gain more insights to take our place in God's grace plan for us. The message of grace should not only excite you, but it should also incite you to take responsibility by faith to align with all God has destined you to be. Without grace, you cannot be all God has called you to be or do what God has called you to do. Grace is more than just a concept; it's a power. It's the power of God at work in you. It is God's ability at work in you when you have no ability. Grace is an expression of God's great love towards us. It is an expression of God's goodness towards undeserving people.

Living a Grace-Centred Life is designed to open you up to what grace has done for you and expose you to the practicality of living a graced life on earth. Your life shall continually be an expression of God's grace as you explore the content of grace in this book in Jesus name. Get ready for a breath-taking view of what God has designed for you in His grace. May God bless you really well as you read along.

PRE-CHAPTER NOTE
Your New Life Identity with Christ

Who are you?
Are you what you do?
Are you what you have achieved?
Are you a product of what you have done right?
Or are you defined by the things you have done wrong?
Are you a Saint or a sinner?
Are you defined by your hurts, past failures or pains?
Are you what others think about you?
Are you *all* of the above? *None* of the above?
Who are you really?

Your approach to life is determined by a clear-cut understanding of your identity.

Prior to the fall of Adam, he looked to God for his esteem and value.

> *Therefore if any man be in Christ, he is a new creature: old things are passed away; behold, all things are become new.*
> II CORINTHIANS 5:17

> *For he hath made him to be sin for us, who knew no sin; that we might be made the righteousness of God in him.*
> II CORINTHIANS 5:21

INTRODUCTION

If any man be in Christ he is a new creature, a brand-new person. Jesus identified with you in your sinful state, and you identified with him in righteousness.

Whatever you identify with will shape or form your identity. Who you identify with will determine your own identity. Identity was stolen by Satan in the garden, and what Satan did in Adam had a great effect on every human being. What Jesus did had a greater effect. Two individuals that have profoundly affected mankind are Adam and Jesus Christ. Who are you identifying with: Adam or Jesus Christ?

What is Identity? Identity is the distinguishing character or personality of an individual. (Merriam-Webster Online, 2017). It is your individuality.

You have an identification with Christ. You must be renewed to it. Identification means to be identical or closely associated with. It means oneness. Your true identity is with Christ. You are in union with Him. As He is, so are you now!

The power of the Christian life is being renewed in the Spirit of your mind to what Jesus did. Be renewed to your new identification after Jesus. Jesus became sin by the power and will of God, but not because He sinned. He was made sin by our sin (yours and mine) so that you could become the righteousness of God. You didn't commit acts of righteousness and holiness to be made righteous. You have been made righteous by the power and will of God.

> *For ye know the grace of our Lord Jesus Christ, that, though he was rich, yet for your sakes he became poor, that ye through his poverty might be rich.*
> II CORINTHIANS 8:9

He became poor that you and I can be rich in Christ.

You have an identification with Adam that brought you death, sin, condemnation, guilt, sickness, disease, poverty, and judgement. You have an identification now with Christ that has brought you life, righteousness, blessings, justification, and prosperity.

You are the blessed of the Lord!

You are the righteousness of God!

You are the justified, but the devil is trying to make you feel guilty.

You are the glorified, but the devil is trying to make you feel ashamed.

You are the beautified, but the devil is trying to make you look ugly. You are extremely valuable, but the devil is trying to make you feel worthless.

You are accepted in the Beloved, but the devil is trying to make you feel rejected and neglected.

You are eternally loved and totally forgiven. You are a brand-new creation. Your new birth (being born again) gave birth to a new you. You are God's treasured possession. You belong to the King of Kings. You are joint heir with Jesus Christ (Romans 8:17). You are a child of God. You are God's workmanship. You are God's masterpiece. You are a success. You are prosperous. You are a product of grace!

> *But ye are a chosen generation, a royal priesthood, an holy nation, a peculiar people; that ye should shew forth the praises of him who hath called you out of darkness into his marvellous light;*
> I Peter 2:9

Please note that the cross was the end of a race (the human race) in Adam and a new race began that I call the *Grace Race*. What transpired at the cross was more than the death of just an innocent man (Jesus). It was your identification, your salvation, your vindication, your justification. It was God redeeming you back to Himself without your works and releasing His supernatural power in your life to live in this new era of grace. Grace is more than just a concept; it is the power of God at work in your life. What happened on the cross was a display of grace. In my first book, I defined grace explicitly. We know the definition of grace. It is important for us to know how to find grace, how to receive of the grace of God and how to apply it in practical ways to our lives. It's impossible for you to be all God has called you to be without the grace of God. Grace is what you need to live all facets of your Christian life. Follow me to the next chapter as we explore *how* to find grace.

Chapter 1
FINDING GRACE

*Let us therefore come boldly unto the throne of grace,
that we may obtain mercy, and **find grace** to help in time of need.*
Hebrews 4:16

It's not enough to know that grace is available; you must find it and maximise it. You need to know how to receive of God's power, God's ability made perfect in human weakness (Grace).

And he said unto me, My grace is sufficient for thee: for my strength is made perfect in weakness. Most gladly therefore will I rather glory in my infirmities, that the power of Christ may rest upon me.
II Corinthians 12:9

Grace brought you salvation and ensures you are endued with God's ability to live this Christian life. You can't be what God has called you to be and do what God has called you to do without His grace. It is God's grace that saves us. You came into the Kingdom of God by grace through faith. You could not save yourself, God's grace saved you. You could not change yourself. Grace changed you through faith. Your salvation was by simple faith in who Jesus is and what He has done. The finished work of Christ gave birth to a new you.

Can you see that you are a product of grace now that you are saved? Are you basking in God's grace? How do you multiply this grace? How do you locate more of it? According to Hebrews 4:16, grace must be found; you have to look for it and acquire it. Grace is at the throne. Jesus has established the throne of grace for us. It's our responsibility to go all out for it.

If you need grace, you must go to the throne of grace. The address of grace is at the throne. Grace is located there, and it's abundant. Jesus has made all grace abound towards us.

> *Moreover the law entered, that the offence might abound.*
> *But where sin abounded, grace did much more abound:*
> ROMANS 5:20

You can get whatever grace you want. The innumerable aspects of God's grace are present at the throne of grace. You did not earn this treasure of grace. You did not deserve it, it was a product of the love of your Heavenly Father. Jesus made it happen, but you must get it yourself. You have a role in finding this grace. Not everyone has found the grace of salvation, but it's available to everyone.

> *For the grace of God that bringeth salvation*
> *hath appeared to all men,*
> TITUS 2:11

Saving grace has appeared to all men but has not been received by all men because not everyone has found it. You that are born-again have found the saving grace of God. You have come to the knowledge of who Jesus is and what He has done for you, and you have believed Him. Saving grace is not all there is to grace; it is but one aspect of the manifold grace of God. What brought you into the Kingdom of Heaven is what will also guarantee your establishment, settlement, provisions, and enablement. That, of course, is grace.

Grace saves you and sustains you. Grace picks you up from the ground level and keeps you standing. Grace is a huge package that has all your needs in it, but you must go get it. God planned everything you will ever need in His grace agenda to guarantee your rest on every side. The level of grace you will enjoy is largely determined by the level of grace you have found. Somebody humorously once said, "Salvation is free, but you have to buy a Bible," (author unknown). Grace is free, but you have the responsibility to find it and mix faith with it. You are not working to earn it; your work now is the work of receiving and believing.

Let's see what we can liken the grace of God to in your quest for it.

> *Again, the kingdom of heaven is like unto treasure hid in a field; the which when a man hath found, he hideth, and for joy thereof goeth and selleth all that he hath, and buyeth that field.*
> MATTHEW 13:44

Notice that a man finds a treasure in a field, but he can't buy the treasure because it's worth more than what he can pay for. He was just privileged to find it. He did not earn the treasure. He did not deserve the treasure, but he had to buy the field where the treasure was found. He had to sell out all he had. He recognised the value of the treasure and that there was a price to pay to acquire the treasure. Grace is that way, we can't earn it, we don't deserve it, but we have to find it. Once we do, we gain the power of God to be what He has called us to be, the ability of God when we don't have any ability, the strength of God when we don't have any strength, and the salvation of God when we can't save ourselves. Our joy becomes full like the man that found the treasure in the field because we discover something valuable. Then we can be willing to do whatever it will take to receive of that grace in our lives.

God loved you and saved you freely; it cost Him His precious Son Jesus Christ. It did not cost you anything. But in another sense, it cost you everything, meaning it cost you your life. You must lose your life to find His life. You have to let go of your old self to identify with Him. It cost you your whole life (old nature) to receive His life (new nature).

> *Then said Jesus unto his disciples, If any man will come after me,*
> *let him deny himself, and take up his cross, and follow me.*
> *For whosoever will save his life shall lose it: and whosoever will lose*
> *his life for my sake shall find it. For what is a man profited, if he*
> *shall gain the whole world, and lose his own soul? or what shall a*
> *man give in exchange for his soul?*
> MATTHEW 16:24-26

> *And he said to them all, If any man will come after me,*
> *let him deny himself, and take up his cross daily, and follow me.*
> *For whosoever will save his life shall lose it: but whosoever will lose*
> *his life for my sake, the same shall save it.*
> LUKE 9:23-24

In the Kingdom, the way to find life is to lose your own life. That's why when you are born again, you lose your own opinions about things and take on God's opinions. The reason is simply. The life you now live is not your life, it's His life. You totally deny self and follow Him. You lose your will to His will; you give up your pride to follow Him. You let go of everything else to receive this life. It's worth giving up everything. The man in Matthew 13:44 sold all that he had to buy the field. Likewise, you must be totally sold out to the Word of Grace. It's a field of treasure that you need to explore.

> *Now therefore, I pray thee, if I have found grace in thy sight,*
> *shew me now thy way, that I may know thee, that I may find grace*
> *in thy sight: and consider that this nation is thy people.*
> *And he said, My presence shall go with thee,*
> *and I will give thee rest.*
> EXODUS 33:13-14

Moses prayed to find grace in the sight of God, knowing that grace guarantees rest. Grace always culminates in rest for everyone that requests it. Moses was given the task to lead the people of Israel, but he saw how inadequate a man could be in leadership without grace, so he asked God to show him His way. Knowing God's way will allow you to accomplish the task or to overcome the situation. Even when you are qualified for the job, you still need grace to get it. Even when you think you can surmount that temptation, you still need grace to ensure victory. It is gross arrogance before God to take grace for granted when you go for that interview thinking you can get the job on your own because you are qualified. Or maybe you have an examination to write. If you refuse to ask for grace to come out with flying colours, even if you have read, you may fail because you did not stick to grace for success. Go to the throne to find grace to help at any time, in any situation, and you will find grace to prevail. Grace is the superb qualifier of the humble; it qualifies the unqualified and also qualifies the qualified. If grace certifies you qualified, then you are truly qualified forever, no matter your actual human credentials.

> *But Noah found grace in the eyes of the Lord.*
> GENESIS 6:8

In the time of Noah, the whole world was wicked and evil. The world was full of atrocities; people's imaginations were corrupted. They committed all sorts of sins, but this Scripture said profoundly that Noah found grace in the eyes of the Lord. The grace of God was available to others, but only Noah found this grace. The Lord intended to wipe out the whole earth, but Noah found grace and was preserved. Dear Valued Ones, grace can be found. You just have to find it. The Lord preserved Noah to protect the root through which the righteous seed (Jesus) would be born and to redeem and restore mankind back to Himself. Glory to God!

THE TRIPOD STAND OF GRACE

Grace stands on three legs like a tripod. There are three platforms to find grace. Grace can be found in this tripod stand. You rise and stand by grace. Grace not only saves you but ensures you are standing. Grace secures your continuous stand with God until the second coming of Christ. If you know these three legs of grace, you will know how to live in this life, how to be empowered to live above sin, and how to receive God's power, ability and strength to become all God has called you to be. You cannot live a life pleasing to God without grace.

> *Therefore being justified by faith,*
> *we have peace with God through our Lord Jesus Christ:*
> *By whom also we have access by faith into this grace wherein we*
> *stand, and rejoice in hope of the glory of God.*
> ROMANS 5:1-2

Our justification was by faith in what Jesus has done. It gave us peace with God. We are saved by grace through faith, and we are to stand by the same grace. We stand by grace through faith. How do we then stand? Where can we find the tripod stand of grace to maintain a proper standing with God and enjoy all the provisions He has made available for us?

THE CROSS

Grace is found at the cross. The cross is the grace of God. It's the power of God. The cross was a display of the grace of God. It is the power of God made perfect in human weakness. The preaching of the cross brings power, God's ability to live right. It was a display of God's wisdom to put you in power over the affairs of life. Salvation is a product of the cross. The more you hear about the cross, the more grace is built inside you.

> *For the preaching of the cross is to them that perish foolishness;*
> *but unto us which are saved it is the power of God.*
> I CORINTHIANS 1:18

Whatever promotes the cross promotes grace. Grace is found at the cross. The preaching of the cross is the unleashing of the power content of grace. The revelation of what transpired at the cross triggers an outpouring of grace. You find more grace from the cross.

Paul talked about the Gospel and showed how that the Gospel is the death, burial and the resurrection of Jesus Christ. Let's look at the account from the book of Acts and from I Corinthians.

> *But none of these things move me, neither count I my life dear unto myself, so that I might finish my course with joy, and the ministry, which I have received of the Lord Jesus, to testify the Gospel of the grace of God.*
> ACTS 20:24

> *Moreover, brethren, I declare unto you the Gospel which I preached unto you, which also ye have received, and wherein ye stand; By which also ye are saved, if ye keep in memory what I preached unto you, unless ye have believed in vain. For I delivered unto you first of all that which I also received, how that Christ died for our sins according to the scriptures; And that he was buried, and that he rose again the third day according to the scriptures:*
> I CORINTHIANS 15:1-4

Correlating these two Scriptures, you will notice that Paul talked about the Gospel of grace and preached of how Jesus died for our sins and was buried and rose again on the third day. This gave birth to the Gospel, the power to live the life to which the cross gave birth, and helped us realise why Jesus had to be punished, why He died, and rose again. As understanding comes to you, the ability and power to live the Christian life are naturally released to you. When you preach the cross to the unsaved, the Holy Spirit pricks their hearts, convinces them, convicts them of sin and converts them from death to life.

Jesus took on the sins of the whole world when He hung on the cross. The cross brings power that enables us to live this Christian life.

Jesus died on the cross, saved you on the cross, healed you on the cross, took your shame on the cross, broke the backbone of sin on the cross, gave you His righteousness on the cross, and transferred His wealth to you on the cross. It was the greatest thing that ever happened to man. It was the greatest event ever recorded. It was the greatest display of God's power. Unconditional love was displayed and released at the cross. Your old man was nailed to the cross; a brand-new you was birthed with the grace for you to excel in life. Your destiny was released. Your blessings were released right there at the cross. This was to ensure that you don't struggle for the blessings anymore, you just faith your way through. You just go to get what has been made yours.

As a Christian, the works of your total salvation and provisions were finished at the cross. Your Christ life was established there, and you are only emerging into what He has made you to be by the Cross. You are not struggling to be. You have been made already. You are evolving to be. The cross was the end of the human race; it gave birth to the Grace Race. When the cross is preached, there is a supernatural release of God's power (grace). Your justification, your vindication, and your identification are hinged on the cross.

THE REVELATION OF JESUS

Grace is found by the revelation of Jesus. Jesus is grace personified. He is the epitome of grace. You can't take Jesus out of the equation of grace. Jesus is grace. The more revelation of Jesus you know, the more graceful you become. You cannot know the intents of grace without knowing the person of grace which is Jesus Christ. Having a revelation of Jesus is inevitable in finding grace. More grace is accorded to those who seek to know the Lord more. More of Him means more of grace. More of you Lord!

And ye shall seek me, and find me,
when ye shall search for me with all your heart.
JEREMIAH 29:13

Seek the Lord with all your heart, and you will find Him. That means you will find grace. Jesus is full of grace and truth:

> *And the Word was made flesh, and dwelt among us,*
> *(and we beheld his glory, the glory as of the only begotten*
> *of the Father,) full of grace and truth.*
> JOHN 1:14

The Word of Grace was made flesh to become the person of grace. Jesus is the Word of God, the more of Him you know, the more grace you acquire. You must seek to find. Grace is found in a relationship with God. The main essence of grace is relationship, not religion. Why go for things instead of pursuing after the embodiment of all things? You will find all facets of grace in Him. Please note that in Him we live, move and have our very being:

> *For in him we live, and move, and have our being; as certain also*
> *of your own poets have said, For we are also his offspring.*
> ACTS 17:28

We cannot exist without Him. We are living by grace through faith. He defines our lives. He is the environment for life. He sustains us. He is our supply.

> *Wherefore gird up the loins of your mind, be sober,*
> *and hope to the end for the grace that is to be brought unto you at*
> *the revelation of Jesus Christ;*
> I PETER 1:13

This Scripture tells us that the grace of God is brought to us by the revelation of Jesus. That's why when you go to church and Jesus is truly taught and magnified, no matter what is preached, it comes back to Jesus and about Jesus, and you are changed. You are edified. You are strengthened. There is a supernatural release of God's power that transforms your life. It might be unexplainable, but its effect is undeniable. That's the power of grace at work. It births testimonies. That's grace!

When you have a revelation of Jesus (who He is, what He did and where he is), you will discover who you are now in Him. When you know what He did, you will begin to maximise it in your life. When you know He lives in you and it is no longer you that lives but Christ that's living in you, that is when power is released.

> *I am crucified with Christ: nevertheless I live; yet not I, but Christ liveth in me: and the life which I now live in the flesh I live by the faith of the Son of God, who loved me, and gave himself for me.*
> GALATIANS 2:20

> *Grace and peace be multiplied unto you through the knowledge of God, and of Jesus our Lord,*
> II PETER 1:2

Grace is multiplied through the knowledge of Jesus. How do I get more grace? How do I multiply grace? How do I increase in grace? The answers are through the knowledge of Jesus. Let there be a craving in your heart to know Jesus more.

> *That I may know him, and the power of his resurrection, and the fellowship of his sufferings, being made conformable unto his death;*
> PHILIPPIANS 3:10

Desire to know Him. That's where the power of the Christian life lies. Paul with all the abundance of revelation still said, "That I may know him and the power of his revelation." That is because he knew that was how he can get more grace. There is no end to knowing Him since there is no end to growing in grace. The more of Him you know, the more you change levels in grace, which is God's supernatural power in human weakness, God's ability when you don't have any ability, God's strength, and provisions.

THE THRONE

> *Let us therefore come boldly unto the throne of grace, that we may obtain mercy, and find grace to help in time of need.*
> HEBREWS 4:16

There are moments of need for everyone, times when we don't know what to do, or how to navigate a situation. The best thing to do is to turn to the throne of grace. Evangelist Billy Graham once said, "When we come to the end of ourselves, we come to the beginning of God." That implies that when we can't help ourselves, we should turn everything over to God. He will step in to deliver and strengthen us. He is our present help in time of need (Psalm 46:1). You cannot live on yesterday's grace. There is manifold grace available at any time, but you have to go get it in a time of need. You cannot overcome temptation in your human strength or with the same pattern with which you overcame it last time. You must go for fresh grace. Don't assume it, acquire it. If you address the issues of life casually, you may end up a casualty. There is always a time of need for every man born of a woman, there will always be the time you need to meet those needs, and you need help. You need grace for each need to be met. You need the grace to match the situation. That grace is available in abundance at the throne of grace. Don't rest and rely on yesterday's grace, go for fresh grace today.

People fall to temptation because they fail to go and get the grace for that temptation. They depend on last month's revival to experience victory in today's challenges. Every time you need grace, go to the throne, and you will find grace to help. Pray your way through that situation. Grace through faith can handle any situation. There is nothing bigger than God, and the God of all grace has made all grace abound towards you. If you ask not, you receive not. If you seek not, you find not. This grace is found in your relationship with God. You should know how to relate to Him concerning any challenge. He responds with power to put you in charge of that situation. That's grace! Grace enthrones you. You confront things that confront you by grace. You cannot overcome the trials of life without the grace of God. You cannot overcome temptations of this life in the energy of the flesh. Grace came to put an end to your struggles. All you need is to labour in prayer. You either choose to labour in human strength to achieve what you want to achieve, or you labour in the prayer of faith at the throne of grace. Either way there is labour involved. Labouring at the throne of grace is profitable, the other is full of weariness. If you choose grace, your labour is no longer after the flesh. Stop striving to prevail over things you can overcome on your knees. Those who depend on grace in times of need will never go to an early grave.

Grace saves you from every problem. Supernatural strength is found at the throne of grace when you don't have any strength. God's ability to do all God has called you to do is found at the throne of grace. Divine power to win against sin is found at the throne of grace. Grace for unusual supply is available at the throne of grace. Your provisions are found at the throne of grace.

Looking unto Jesus the author and finisher of our faith; who for the joy that was set before him endured the cross, despising the shame, and is set down at the right hand of the throne of God.
HEBREWS 12:2

Jesus endured the cross; He despised the shame. He finished the work of our total salvation. Now He sits at the right hand of the throne of grace which is the throne of God. He advocates our case at the throne. Once we appear helpless in our human strength, we go to the throne of grace, and He helps us with the needed grace. He knows what you are going through, He was here before and has experienced life here on earth. He feels your struggles and ensures you are not alone, that you are helped, and that help comes from the throne when you make a request for it. You only receive what you need. Your desire is your requirement to acquire more grace. If you need it, then you must go for it. He despised the shame so that you will know no shame in this life. Jesus completed the work for our lifting, for our breakthrough, for our success, for our glorious destiny. He did it over two thousand years ago. You can't afford to remain in that challenge that has been handled already by grace. Go for grace!

TAKE AWAY DECLARATIONS

I have the power of God in me. I grow in power as I grow in the grace of God.

The cross of Jesus Christ has released the power of God in me, and I increase in my knowledge of what Jesus has done for me.

I identify with Jesus and what He did for me at the cross. As He is, so am I now. I'm identical with Christ. You can't differentiate us. I'm in union with Him. (I John 1:17.)

I receive grace to know You more than ever before, Holy Ghost reveal Jesus in me, to me and through me to my world. (Philippians 3:10, Galatians 1:16 and Ephesians 1:17.)

I go to the throne of grace with confidence, to obtain mercy and find grace to help in time of need . (Hebrews 4:16.)

I don't approach the throne of grace with guilt in my heart because I have been justified by God's grace.

PRE-CHAPTER POEM
Sure Flight, Sure Destination

There is a sure flight; it's a flight on the wings of God's grace

There is a sure destination; it's a place of rest

Without grace, you have no feather to fly

There are other flights, but they can develop mechanical faults

No flight is as sure as the Grace flight

The wings of God's grace are the surest flight to take

This flight is failure-proof, it can never fail

It's a reliable flight; you can count on it any day at anytime

Get on board on a graceful flight

Your boarding ticket is your faith

All expenses have been paid for by Christ Jesus

The wings of God's grace are the surest flight

that guarantees a sure destination.

Chapter 2
MIXING FAITH WITH THE WORD OF GRACE

*Let us therefore fear, lest, a promise being left us of entering into his rest, any of you should seem to come short of it. For unto us was the gospel preached, as well as unto them: but the word preached did not profit them, not being **mixed with faith** in them that heard it.*
HEBREWS 4:1-2

The word *fear* as used here implies being careful, or being afraid of losing something. In other words, let us, therefore, be careful not to miss out on God's promises. The Word of God is God's grace in print. A compendium of grace makes up the Word of God.

And now, brethren, I commend you to God, and to the word of his grace, which is able to build you up, and to give you an inheritance among all them which are sanctified.
ACTS 20:32

You have to be careful because it can slip out of your hands, if not mixed with faith.

What is rest? Rest is when you desist from your work and relax to enjoy the fruits of the work done. Jesus Christ has done the work. Enjoy the fruit of the work He has done for you. You are to rely on the finished work of Christ on the cross through faith. Paul preached the Gospel, but the Word did not profit all his listeners because they did not mix it with faith when they heard it. Faith remains a non-negotiable requirement to explore the profit in God's grace. God's Word is a conveyor of God's grace. Whenever God speaks to us, He speaks graceful words. Faith is what you need to convert God's word into profit for you. The Word cannot profit you if you don't mix it with faith.

God does not speak void words. Each word he speaks is meant to profit us. When God speaks to us, there is power inside every word to produce after its kind. When He speaks success, there is power in that word to produce the success required. When He speaks prosperity, there is power in that word to produce that prosperity. When He speaks healing, there is power available in that word to cause healing. When He speaks righteousness, there is power available to make us live righteously.

God's personality and integrity are tied to His Word. He is speaking Grace to us which is the totality of the finished work of Christ Jesus. GRACE is *God's Reliable Abundance by Christ's Effort*. We are meant to respond to grace through faith, which converts every Word of Grace into profit! The mixer that mixes the Word with faith is your heart. Your heart is the bedrock of faith.

> *That if thou shalt confess with thy mouth the Lord Jesus, and shalt believe in thine heart that God hath raised him from the dead, thou shalt be saved. For with the heart man believeth unto righteousness; and with the mouth confession is made unto salvation.*
> ROMANS 10:9-10

God's Word becomes impotent in your life if you lack the faith to mix the Word. God's Word is full of potent abilities (grace) to cause change in your life, but you must exercise faith to draw from this potency. The Word of God is full of living power.

Just as faith comes by hearing God's Word, so also grace comes by hearing the Word. The two must mix properly to produce the desired result. The blending of grace and faith is the key to profitable living.

What is mixing?

Mixing is a broad term in baking that generally means to combine two or more ingredients lightly together. According to Robert Blakeslee, author of "Your Time to Cook," most often you will mix baking ingredients by stirring them with a spoon or fork. You must continue to stir the ingredients until they are "evenly distributed," Blakeslee states. For heavier mixing, some cooks use an electric hand mixer or a kitchen stand mixer to speed the process. (From http://www.livestrong.com/article/431388-what-is-the-difference-between-mix-beat-in-baking/)

Once your ingredients have been selected and measured, often the next step is to mix them all together. Mixing serves to physically break apart the proteins in the flour into smaller pieces and expose the moisture-loving portions of the recipes, so the two blend together more effectively. Mixing is a general term that includes stirring, beating, blending, binding, creaming, whipping and folding. During mixing, two or more ingredients are evenly dispersed in one another until they become one product.

(From http://www.craftybaking.com/howto/mixing-method-basics)

After gathering your ingredients from the Word of Grace, you must endeavour to add faith to them and then mix effectively until you get your desired product. The mixing process of grace and faith takes place in your heart.

> *Be not carried about with divers and strange doctrines. For it is a good thing that the heart be established with grace;*

> *not with meats, which have not profited them that have been occupied therein.*
> HEBREWS 13:9

> *That if thou shalt confess with thy mouth the Lord Jesus, and shalt believe in thine heart that God hath raised him from the dead, thou shalt be saved. For with the heart man believeth unto righteousness; and with the mouth confession is made unto salvation.*
> ROMANS 10:9-10

Once grace and faith are established in your heart, your testimonies are established already. This mixture is what guarantees that you will profit as a Christian. The binding of grace and faith makes tremendous power available to produce results. The mating of grace and faith breeds possibilities. Nothing stops these two forces from producing. You can't respond to grace through faith and not have results to show for it. The reason the Israelites missed out on the promises of God was their lack of faith. It is essential that we guide our hearts jealously against every form of unbelief because the same heart that harbours faith can also harbour unbelief. Doubt is rooted in the heart and so is faith. You choose which one to work with. The land of Canaan is likened to the land of Grace which God has brought us into today through the finished work of Jesus Christ. It's all grace work. It's a land flowing with milk and honey. A land full of God's goodness. To many it seems too good to be true that it is possible for God to make all things available to us by grace without works. That was the situation the Israelites faced. It seemed too good to be true that God had prepared a most glorious land for every one of them. They doubted God, and by so doing, they missed out on God's provision for them. The Word of God that you don't mix faith cannot do you any good. You cannot benefit from it because you don't believe it. God has prepared a place of rest through grace in Jesus Christ. It's a place of comfort, holiness, fruitfulness, prosperity, enjoyment, righteousness, peace and joy in the Holy Ghost. Just like we had the land of Canaan, this is the land of Grace, and it's only in Christ Jesus. It's the Kingdom of God made manifest on earth for the children of God to explore and enjoy. The tool needed for you to explore and maximise this grace is faith. Without faith, you can have so much available, yet enjoy so little. All you will ever need for every aspect of your life has been made available in Christ Jesus. When you entered into Christ, you entered your place of rest. There you can desist from your labour and struggles and rely on what He accomplished on your behalf. You can take advantage of the opportunity to relax from human toil. God saw how the Israelites struggled and suffered in the land of Egypt, so He made a way of escape for them by sending Moses to deliver and lead them to the Promised Land. A wealthy place was prepared for them to inherit by divine orchestration, a place where He intended to bless them and where they would inherit houses, fields, and land flowing with milk and honey that they did not work for. God did not only intend to bring the children of Israel out of bondage but to ensure they enter into a place of blessing and rest that He had prepared for them (the land of Canaan).

The first generation of the Israelites missed out on God's promises because of their unbelief. Only the generation of those who believed fully in what God had promised and were fully persuaded were allowed to enter the Promised Land.

You can choose to believe in an already made work of Christ and enjoy what He has done or you can reject His work and continue in struggles. The choice is yours! It's advisable to depend solely on what Jesus has done. Jesus did not only bring you out of bondage but to also guaranteed a place of rest for you. God does not want you to just receive salvation and suffer through life in the wilderness but for you to come to a glorious relationship with Him where all His *goodship* is shipped into your life so that you can enjoy God's blessings. Don't settle for the average, don't accept the wilderness as your destination. The Lord has a place of rest that you need to mix with faith to enjoy. Grace is meant to bring you to a wealthy place where there is an abundance and God's sufficiency in all things.

> *For we which have believed do enter into rest, as he said, As I have sworn in my wrath, if they shall enter into my rest: although the works were finished from the foundation of the world.*
> *For he spake in a certain place of the seventh day on this wise, And God did rest the seventh day from all his works.*
> *And in this place again, If they shall enter into my rest.*
> *Seeing therefore it remaineth that some must enter therein, and they to whom it was first preached entered not in because of unbelief: Again, he limiteth a certain day, saying in David, To day, after so long a time; as it is said, To day if ye will hear his voice, harden not your hearts. For if Jesus had given them rest, then would he not afterward have spoken of another day. There remaineth therefore a rest to the people of God. For he that is entered into his rest, he also hath ceased from his own works, as God did from his.*
> *Let us labour therefore to enter into that rest, lest any man fall after the same example of unbelief.*
> HEBREWS 4:3-11

The work of grace has brought us eternal rest. You don't need to live in hardship anymore; you just need to live under His Lordship to enjoy His goodness. Grace life has put an end to hard life. Jesus is not dying again. He died once to bring us into rest. Your own works which include your struggles in the energy of the flesh to please God, and your struggles to achieve things by your physical strength have ended. Stop striving, stop trying to get God to do something. Stop trusting in yourself and your abilities to do things to get God to work things out for you. God has already done everything! He has already supplied everything you will ever need. You can only enter into His finished work by faith when you cease from your own works. God calls every believer to this level of faith with Him; a relationship where you don't have to try to get God to move, force God to move, to do something, or plead or beg Him to do something. You can just rest in the truth that God has already supplied everything you will ever need. Start trusting in God's grace and not in yourself. Your labour is now a labour of faith. Believing enough to receive. God finished the works of creation from the foundation of the world by His Word. What God enjoys today is the fruits of the work done from the beginning. Jesus has done all the work there is to do. You are to enjoy the fruit of His labour by believing. Just as God rested on the seventh day after creation, we are to rest too because Jesus is our Sabbath rest (a place of victory, confidence, safety, security, and enjoyment). We are to rest in His finished works by faith. Your faith is the channel through which the provisions God are made available by the finished works of Christ to flow into all your life endeavours. Without faith, grace lies dormant. Grace is available and faith is all that needs to be added. Your faith is the gateway to grace. You are called to walk in the fullness of grace through faith. Your major labour is a labour to build your faith and to use it to explore the grace of God. Otherwise, you will be like the Israelites who had such a great promise but did not taste of it because of unbelief. You can't afford to have just a glassful of water when the full ocean is available. Grace brought the fullness of God's goodness to mankind. The promise of grace is here, let's make the most of it through faith.

The price paid for your salvation is the same price that secured your all-around success in life. Faith is working with the Word of grace to see your desired result. Faith is putting grace to work, which in turn commits God to make good His promises. Grace is available, but it does not just work on its own. You must have a role to play which is partnering with God by simple child-like faith to see the manifestations of what God has said. If the saving grace that brought salvation did not just fall on your lap. You must believe to be saved. Faith must be mixed with grace to ensure your abundant provision. You will always need faith in every aspect of your life to enjoy grace. It is your responsibility to prove you acknowledge what God has done and what He has provided through His Son Jesus Christ. It is expedient that we recognise that our faith is not trying to make God do what He has already done for us via the finished works of Christ Jesus. It is knowing the entitlement we have by grace and simply walking in it by faith. Grace is what gives validity and substance to our faith. Exercising our faith without grace would be futile because faith must be bound with grace to produce what we want.

Exercise your faith, it is your currency, while grace is what you need to buy. If you have the currency and you know what is available in the market, you won't find it difficult to go shopping. The more currency you have, the more goods you can buy. It is the same with faith and grace. If you are deficient in currency, you will be limited in what to buy. The problem will not be with the shopping centre, but with the buyer who needs to increase his or her currency.

God has made all grace abound towards you by what Christ has done. He is resting and expecting you to acquire as much as you can by as much currency (faith) you can gather from the Word (Grace + Faith). Your faith will determine what level of grace you will enjoy. God has done His part. Your faith will deliver your provisions to you. When the devil comes in to steal from you or deprive you of your goodness in Christ, your faith is your weapon of war. It is your defence. Faith is you resting in the finished work of Christ. Christ has already done a finished work on your behalf; you need to use your faith to draw the physical manifestations into your life.

THE PROCESS OF MIXING THE WORD OF GRACE WITH FAITH

There is a process of mixing that will culminate in your profiting from the Word. It is the sequence for profitability from the Word of grace. Your profits stem from this process. Every Word of Grace is a word decked with profits, but the profits become manifest for all to see when you properly mix faith with them. Let's see the profit sequence that delivers results when we examine the Word.

MEDITATE ON THE WORD

> *Meditate upon these things; give thyself wholly to them;*
> *that thy profiting may appear to all.*
> I TIMOTHY 4:15

Meditate on the things you hear. Your meditation is what showcases your profit in the Word to everyone. Nobody knows how much you have read until they know how much you can think by your results. To meditate simply means to think (ponder) carefully on something. Your thinking makes your results thicker and noticeable by all. It puts your result on a hill that cannot be hidden.

Meditation produces profit for everybody to see. Meditation is required for the Word to produce tangible results. Meditation is the labour room where understanding is birthed. When there is understanding, faith comes alive. The moment your faith comes alive, your answer is delivered. Understanding is the right interpretation of knowledge. It means you finally know what the Word is talking about. You can now interpret the Word, put yourself in the place of the Word through mental brooding over the Word. The moment you do that, faith surges up in your heart and action hormones are provoked. There is a stirring of your faith to take steps when you start binding faith with the Word of Grace to see what it actually says about you.

Meditation is taking the lid off the Word and ensuring you make the most of the content. Without meditation, you can't access the profitable contents of the Word. The Word of God is like a container that holds everything you will ever need. Each word you hear carries a content of its own. God placed power in every word you hear. The way to open up the content is by meditation. Meditation opens you up to the Word and opens the Word up to you.

This book of the law shall not depart out of thy mouth; but thou shalt meditate therein day and night, that thou mayest observe to do according to all that is written therein: for then thou shalt make thy way prosperous, and then thou shalt have good success.

JOSHUA 1:8

It's amazing that many Christian think being born again is an automatic walk into success or a righteous, holy, and prosperous life. No, it's not automatic! It's just a welcome note to the world of success, prosperity, and holiness. There is the place of mind renewal. You must be renewed to these things because your mind was not born again, only your spirit was. We will talk more on this as we go on. You have to do the work of getting the Word of God into your heart. Out of the abundance of the heart, the mouth speaks.

> *A good man out of the good treasure of his heart bringeth forth that which is good; and an evil man out of the evil treasure of his heart bringeth forth that which is evil: for of the abundance of the heart his mouth speaketh.*
> LUKE 6:45

When the Word is in your heart, your mouth will naturally speak about, and your life will go in that direction. Meditate on the Word day and night (Joshua 1:8). Nurture your mind, impute the Word and let your mind conform to your new status to make it visible on the outside. It's a work within that reveals your heart on the outside. When you meditate on the Word, understanding is birthed, and faith comes alive. Then you know exactly what to do, and you do it; you become prosperous and have good success. Success is the outcome or profit of meditating on the Word. When you say a business was a huge success, it means that the business had great financial profitability. The words *good success* here mean good profits or good gain. It only comes by meditating on the Word and determining to do what the Word says. Without meditation, you won't know what to do, and without doing (action), your faith is dead. Then there is no result.

BELIEVE THE WORD UNRESERVEDLY

After meditating on the Word, your faith is awakened. Keep your faith intact. Guide against unbelief. Believe God's Word completely without any element of doubt, without restraint and withholding nothing. Have no alternative to the Word you have heard. Let it be the final say in all situations. Hold on to it, don't give up on the Word for any reason. Don't allow doubt to creep in. Fight every iota of doubt to keep your faith in a full gear to deliver your result. Shun doubt and build your faith up. If you win the battle against doubt in your mind, you win the battle against limitations in life. Doubters live in a world of negativity, but believers live in a world of no limits. You might not look like what the Word is saying now, but that's why the Word came in the first place to make you exactly what it says you are. Believe it until you see it. The world's system is *seeing is believing*, but God's system is *believing is seeing*. You cannot receive what you have not believed for. You are only entitled to see what you have believed and seen from the Word of God's grace. The process of waiting on the Word through faith is a mixing process. You are blending your faith with the Word to see your product well-baked. The more you mix the Word with faith without changing your mind or doubting the Word, the more glorious your product will be.

> *For verily I say unto you, That whosoever shall say unto this mountain, Be thou removed, and be thou cast into the sea; and shall not doubt in his heart, but shall believe that those things which he saith shall come to pass; he shall have whatsoever he saith.*
> MARK 11:23

Saying it with your mouth, believing it in your heart and eliminating every doubt is what produces your desired results. When you believe that what you say shall come to pass, then you will have whatsoever you say come to pass. God is committed to the belief system in your heart in response to your prayers. Totally believe God in your heart and totally neglect every doubt. Shut down your doubt system and power on your belief system. There is always a battle for each word you hear from God. The devil will always come to question the Word and to create doubt. That was the trick he used on Eve.

> *Now the serpent was more subtil than any beast of the field which the Lord God had made. And he said unto the woman, Yea, hath God said, Ye shall not eat of every tree of the garden?*
> GENESIS 3:1

The serpent's words caused Eve to think and doubt set into her heart. She started doubting what God told her, and was considering what the devil had said. The devil still questions people about the Word and tries to create doubt. He wants to make room for a lie and paint you a lie so God's Word will not be the final say. But if you know what God has said and you stick to it no matter what, the devil will gradually give up and allow you to enjoy what God has said is yours. I see you enjoying God's promises to the fullest in Jesus name. Amen! An end has come to every deception of the devil in Jesus name.

Why do you need to believe the Word? You need to believe God's Word because God is worth His Word. Whatever God says, He is able to do. God's Word has the ability to accomplish whatever God pleases, but your belief in the Word is what delivers the result.

> *So shall my word be that goeth forth out of my mouth: it shall not return unto me void, but it shall accomplish that which I please, and it shall prosper in the thing whereto I sent it.*
> ISAIAH 55:11

The Word of God prospers in that area of your life to which God has sent it. Isaiah 55:11 explains that each word that God releases from His mouth is a word with content to deliver your expectations. God does not speak empty words. His words do not return to Him void, they accomplishes His desires. His Word contains life, health, peace, prosperity, success, joy, and righteousness. God's Word has something in it for your lifting, breakthrough, and deliverance. You can count on the Word of God at any time. It cannot fail, and it can't return to God empty, it must accomplish its assignment in your life. Every word has a purpose to accomplish your life.

GIVE YOURSELF WHOLLY TO THE WORD

Meditate upon these things; give thyself wholly to them; that thy profiting may appear to all.
I Timothy 4:15

Give thyself completely to the Word of God. For your profit to appear to all after meditating and believing the Word, you must also give your entire being to the Word. The Word you don't pay attention to cannot profit you. Go full length with the Word of God. Increase your capacity to generate greater faith by giving yourself to the details in the Word. Being sold out to the Word of God will cause you to stand out in life. Know what the Word is saying concerning that pressing issue. Know more about the provisions that grace has made available for you and bind your faith with it.

Ho, every one that thirsteth, come ye to the waters, and he that hath no money; come ye, buy, and eat; yea, come, buy wine and milk without money and without price. Wherefore do ye spend money for that which is not bread? and your labour for that which satisfieth not? hearken diligently unto me, and eat ye that which is good, and let your soul delight itself in fatness. Incline your ear, and come unto me: hear, and your soul shall live; and I will make an everlasting covenant with you, even the sure mercies of David.
Isaiah 55:1-3

Everything you will ever need is available in the Word. You don't need money to make purchases here. All you need is a diligent pursuit of the Word. Hunger for the Word. Just be thirsty, and you will be filled. Without a sold-out commitment to the Word, it will be difficult to draw out virtues from it. Labour for that which can give satisfaction, which is the Word. Eat the Word; it will make you fat and flourishing. Delight thy soul in the fatness of the Word. Commit your soul to the Word of God.

> *Buy the truth, and sell it not; also wisdom,*
> *and instruction, and understanding.*
> PROVERBS 23:23

What does it mean to buy the truth? It simply means to give yourself wholly to the Word of God, to be totally sold-out to the truth. Just like you give currency in exchange for goods, you should give your life in exchange for the Word. Do whatever it will take to give total attention to the Word. It also means to lean your entire personality on God's Word in absolute trust and confidence in His power, wisdom, and goodness. It's a part of the process of mixing the Word with faith. It's a point of no going back. I will hold to the Word till my change comes. Get to the point where the totality of your being has been given to the Word completely; give yourself away to the Word.

BE A WORD PRACTITIONER

> *Yea, a man may say, Thou hast faith,*
> *and I have works: shew me thy faith without thy works,*
> *and I will shew thee my faith by my works.*
> JAMES 2:18

Grace does not work by itself; faith puts grace to work. Show your works to prove your belief. The proof of faith is action. Do something with the Word of God you have received. There are many Word-filled believers but only a few action-filled believers. Knowing the Word is not enough, you must do something with the Word you know. Practice what you believe. Be a perpetual doer. If you believe what grace has provided, then act it and see the manifestations in your life. You don't go to bed with your belief; you go to work with your belief. You believe you are healed, then act it. You believe you have been made the righteousness of God in Christ Jesus, then act it. You believe you are blessed, then act it. You believe you are prosperous, then do what you need to do to enjoy and see the prosperity. Covenant practices like tithing are avenues to prove you believe when it comes to prosperity. It means you know that He has made all grace abound and you are proving Him in remembrance of His promises. Then you see God at work. Faith is a work you must do to see the result you want. It's not enough to have faith but to work your faith to produce results. Faith must go to work to bring you profit. I believe, and therefore I do. You must believe and do to see results. Faith is an action word. You must act faith.

> *For as the body without the spirit is dead,*
> *so faith without works is dead also.*
> JAMES 2:26

Faith is not just believing in what God can do. It is been driven by your belief to do something to show that you really believe. Taking works out of faith is taking life out of faith. Your faith is alive by your works (actions). When the spirit of a man leaves his body that man is considered dead. In the same vein, when works leave your faith, your faith is considered lifeless. Your faith is proven alive by your actions of obedience to the Word of God. God's Word says it, we believe it, and that settles it.

DECLARE THE WORD

> *We having the same spirit of faith,*
> *according as it is written, I believed, and therefore have I spoken;*
> *we also believe, and therefore speak;*
> II CORINTHIANS 4:13

If you believe, then you must speak it. Speaking what you believe is a sign of total conviction. You don't believe God's Word yet if you can't talk about it. Declare what you believe. If you really believe it, then speak it. Verbalise the Word. Sound the Word to live a sound life. Announce the Word to be announced to your world. What you say is what you are qualified to see. Your speech expresses your belief. Professing what you believe is laying hold on your possession. You might not see it in your life now, but professing it brings it into your life. Keep saying it and eventually you will start seeing it. The things you have seen from the Word that you consistently talk about will eventually come into your life. One of the attributes of faith is that it speaks into existence what it believes. Faith thinks, sees, speaks and possesses. This is the delivering point of the profits of the Word of God. What you have meditated upon, what you have believed, what you are totally sold-out to, what you have practiced and declared of the Word of Grace delivers your profits. The process of mixing is a great process that must deliver anytime any day. You can't do all the process mentioned above and not have a good profit. It is my prayer that as you deliberately put into practice what you hear that you will receive your heart's desires in Jesus name.

TAKE AWAY DECLARATIONS

I acknowledge that the Word of God is the Word of Grace and I mix my faith with all the promises that the Word has said concerning me (Acts 20:32 and Acts 20:24).

I meditate on the goodness of the Lord, and I mix my faith with it, thereby having tangible proofs to show (I Timothy 4:15).

I speak to every mountain between me and my place of rest to be removed and cast into the sea in Jesus name (Mark 11:23).

I claim my inheritance by faith. I receive my blessings, I receive my miracles, and I receive my breakthroughs in the name of Jesus.

I take delivery of my miracle job, miracle marriage and my miracle children in the name of Jesus.

God has guaranteed my all-around rest. Whatever is contending with the Word of rest in my life be destroyed in the name of Jesus.

By the power of the Holy Ghost, I contend with every demonic power fighting against by my all-around settlement in Jesus name (Deuteronomy 2:24).

I am restful on every side because Jesus has died for me to experience rest.

Jesus, I desire your grace to rest on your finished work on the cross and not to depend on my struggles for blessings.

What Christ has done for me on the cross finds practical fulfilment in my life as I rely on Him by faith in Jesus name.

PRE-CHAPTER POEM
The Best Formula

The best formula guarantees the best answer

The best formula is worth going for

The best formula simplifies the equation

The best formula delivers easy answers
to the most difficult question

The best formula doesn't complicate the equation;
it solves the equation

The best formula is what you need to know
to get your desired results

If you know how to use the best formula,
you will get the best result

Putting the best formula to work is what ends life's struggles

When you apply the best formula through faith,
your desired result is certain

Grace is the best formula

Chapter 3

PUTTING GRACE TO WORK

Scientist Isaac Newton told us that every object remains at the state of rest until a relevant force is applied to it. This is equally true with grace. Grace will remain dormant if you refuse to put it to work. Acting on grace is what delivers your result. You can't receive grace and do nothing with it. Grace is not only what we receive as children of God, but it is also what we must put to work in our lives. No matter how anointed you are, if you refuse to switch on the light from the switch box in your room, the light will never come up. That does not mean there is no power in the house. The power needed to generate light has been supplied, but you have the responsibility to switch on the light from the switch box. Faith is the switch box; your power supply is grace. If there is power in the house and there is a switch in your room, then there will be light. Your act to switch on the light is an act of faith which triggers the release of grace. These are two powerful components that determine your glory. They are great forces that every Christian must pay attention to. They work dependent on each other. Your switch is useless without a sure supply of power in your house. Having a sure supply of power in your house without a switch to match to enable the light to come up is a waste of time and resources. You must learn how to utilise your faith to get what grace has in store for you. Faith is what turns on the exceeding grace of God. Faith releases the content of grace for profitable living. Faith connects you to the power of grace that clears every challenge out of your way. Nothing stands in the way of faith and grace. When faith is at work, the power content of grace to deliver is in place. All provisions of the Kingdom are released at the expense of grace and dependent on faith to deliver.

> *But we have this treasure in earthen vessels, that the excellency of the power may be of God, and not of us.*
> II CORINTHIANS 4:7

We are full of graceful treasures on our inside as born-again children of God. Child of God, you are not an empty vessel; you are a vessel full of grace. Grace is the treasure of God in our earthen vessel, and this treasure is God's power. It's full of varieties; you need to draw out these treasures from the realm of the unseen to the seen realm. It is God's power made manifest in human weakness. It is God at work in you both to will and to do of His good pleasure (Philippians 2:3). It's God's ability on your inside when you don't have any ability to accomplish all God has called you to accomplish and to be all God has designed you to be. The key to this treasure is faith. When it's not of us, then it is of grace. The excellency of the power of grace is God's prerogative, and He has placed it in our earthen vessels to do exploits. Your faith is what unlocks this treasure box of grace in you. You don't know what you have; you don't know who you are and what power you are made of. You are a product of grace, so don't settle for less. You have been given so much, so make the most of it. Grace has brought you the abundance of all things. Grace is God's sufficiency for you to live a sufficient life.

> *But unto every one of us is given grace according to the measure of the gift of Christ.*
> EPHESIANS 4:7

Notice that grace is given and this grace is multipliable. It's a gift you have received, and you are expected to work with it. Pay attention to what you have received; it's a treasure. The attention you pay to this treasure you have received determines what you will obtain from life. Embrace the grace you have received and maximise it.

> *We then, as workers together with him,*
> *beseech you also that ye receive not the grace of God in vain.*
> *(For he saith, I have heard thee in a time accepted,*
> *and in the day of salvation have I succoured thee: behold, now is the*
> *accepted time; behold, now is the day of salvation.)*
> 2 CORINTHIANS 6:1-2

Grace can be received in vain. Grace can be dormant despite its potency. Notice in the Scripture above that the Word *succour* means assistance in time of difficulty. It means all forms of aid given to you at salvation. This means that grace has been released to assist you in all situations. There is an invisible force helping you, and that is the force of grace. You only need to mix faith with it.

Salvation carried with it all you will ever need to live a glorious life. Salvation is an umbrella word that encompasses your total provisions in Christ. It came with aid for you to go through life. You are not alone, God is helping you through life. It's all grace work. God knows your struggles; He has brought you the solutions. Use what you have been given. You must acknowledge that you have been given grace to actually act as one with grace. You can grow in grace because you can never outgrow God's grace, but you must also realise that you are already in a level of grace. You need to maximise it. Don't let grace be in vain in your life. Grace should have proofs to show. Grace is for work. Start working with the grace you have received. The Scriptures clearly says you should not receive God's grace in vain. In other words, do something with what you have received. Grace should be manifested. It should be with effects. It should produce results. If God has made you righteous, bear the fruits of righteousness. Salvation came with what you need to be righteous. If you have neither made a commitment to be righteous, or you have not acted it by faith, you have no result. Your actions are proofs of your faith, and they give life to the grace upon your life. If God has called you rich, act as one who is rich because the grace has been given for you to become all that God has called you to be. If God says you can live a life of dominion over sin, don't allow sin to enslave you anymore because grace has been given to live above sin. When you stand your ground, you are proofing the grace for that particular thing to work. God will not demand from you what He has not given you the grace to accomplish. Every demand the Lord is requesting from you is as a result of the grace that has been given you to meet that demand. God will not allow a challenge to come your way if He has not given you the grace to overcome it. There is an overcomers' grace in you. Don't appear before any challenge as if you can't handle it, appear as one that has all it takes to handle the problem, and you will emerge victoriously. You have been given all forms of grace to triumph in life. Even if the challenge seems impossible to surmount, it's actually surmountable. You just need more faith to kick it out of the way. Mountains skip at the presence of grace. You carry grace. Speak to every mountain, it will respond to the faith you have mixed with God's grace. Grace has fixed it; you are only featuring in it to claim your victory. Grace has fixed that sickness, go take your healing by faith and act it. Act until you see your desire in your body. Don't let the devil talk you out of your breakthrough, success, or liberty. They are a done deal. We are only receiving the victory of a battle already won. Your battle is a battle to believe to the later until you see your change. I see God delivering your long-awaited breakthrough in your hands in Jesus name.

> *For this thing I besought the Lord thrice,*
> *that it might depart from me. And he said unto me,*
> *My grace is sufficient for thee: for my strength is made perfect in*
> *weakness. Most gladly therefore will I rather glory in my infirmities,*
> *that the power of Christ may rest upon me.*
> II CORINTHIANS 12:8-9

Paul had a particular challenge and sought the face of the Lord three times. It's amazing that God responded to Him by saying, "My grace is sufficient for you, for my strength is made perfect in weakness." Is that not amazing? God did not tell him to go and manage the problem. He did not say endure the problem like that. He said that the grace He had given to Paul is sufficient for him and God's strength was perfected in

Paul's weakness. There are times you have to look inward to gain victory on the outward. What you may be looking for may be lying inside you dormant, just waiting for a trigger to manifest. This is because God allows what you are going through to come to you because He has endued you with grace to overcome it. Remind yourself that you can, and you will be amazed how empowered you are to do it. I believe Paul went out of His prayer room that day with a smile on his face knowing he has been given what it takes to conquer that situation. All he needed was to believe, and that was it. He never complained about that problem in his epistles. God meant here that grace has been made sufficient for all life's challenges. God has empowered you with grace. He wants you to start using it. Remember that Paul was an apostle already before this challenge. A great man of God, still he was faced with some difficulties, trials, and challenges.

*These things I have spoken unto you,
that in me ye might have peace. In the world ye shall have
tribulation: but be of good cheer; I have overcome the world.*
JOHN 16:33

There are no problem-free zones where you can run to in this life. You will be faced with challenges, but victory is guaranteed. That is the reason you carry that grace, it is to address the situation with faith. What you carry is enough for you to conquer. Face the challenge with boldness. Check inwardly; you are endowed with all you need to break through. Grace empowers you. Use what you have by faith to get what you want. Don't run away from challenges, respond to them with grace. You have the grace!

*For whatsoever is born of God overcometh the world: and this is the
victory that overcometh the world, even our faith.*
I JOHN 5:4

We are all a product of grace. We are born of grace. We are world overcomers. No challenge is permitted to throw us off balance. We have been graced to overcome. You have the overcomer's ability on your inside. All you need is to put your faith to work. Grace has saved you and put you in charge of every situation. It has empowered you above every challenge. Do exploits with what you carry.

I can do all things through Christ which strengtheneth me.
PHILIPPIANS 4:13

You can do all things through Christ that gives you the grace to get things done. Grace is God's strength. It is an enabling force that secures your enthronement in anything you do. Don't look at your strength, look at the strength of grace. That is your enabler; the power to behave and become all God desires for you is in grace. Grace is God's ability at work in us.

Wherefore, my beloved, as ye have always obeyed,
not as in my presence only, but now much more in my absence,
work out your own salvation with fear and trembling.
¹³ For it is God which worketh in you
both to will and to do of his good pleasure.
PHILIPPIANS 2:12-13

Salvation, though received, has to be worked out. You must work it out with fear and trembling. In continuation, it said it is God that works in you both to will and to do of His good pleasure. Give diligence to ensure you maximise this power at work in you to work out your salvation. You have to respond to this grace in you. God is at work in you, but you have to work it out. God's working on the inward will require your cooperation of faith to bring about an outward manifestation. There is power in you to do all God has called you to do and to be all God has called you be, but the use of this power lies with you. You determine how far you want to use this power.

TAKE AWAY DECLARATIONS

I can do all things through Christ that strengthens me (Philippians 4:13).

Christ is in me, which is the hope of my glory. I put to work the power of Christ in me (Colossians 1:27).

I take responsibility to put my faith to work by relying solely on God's grace.

The grace of God is sufficient for me, thereby supernatural strength is made perfect in my weakness (II Corinthians 12:8).

The power of God has been made available by virtue of the sufficient grace of God upon me (II Corinthians 12:9).

I do not receive the grace of God in vain; I put grace to work by faith (I Corinthians 6:1).

I am succoured (assisted) by God's grace; I have divine assistance in times of difficulties thereby turning supposed rough rides in life to smooth rides for me (I Corinthians 6:2).

PRE-CHAPTER STORY

THE CATERPILLAR AND THE BUTTERFLY

An ugly looking caterpillar was worried about its appearance. It wanted to fly so quick and so high in the blue sky but did not know how to fly. It had always admired other butterflies with their colourful wings. One day it came across an adult butterfly, and they got talking. He finally poured his heart and asked several questions:

Caterpillar: What do I do? How do I fly? Can I be better than this? Is there anything good in me? Is there more to me? Or is this all I can ever be?

Adult Butterfly: Of course, you can be better, you have all it takes on the inside to be the best of you. You have an inner beauty that the world has not seen yet. The world wants to see the inner you.

Caterpillar: Hmm, I really want to showcase my beauty. I want to be at my best. What do I do?

Adult Butterfly: Nice question, it's a process. You can't become a butterfly overnight. Let me tell you my story of how I became a butterfly. My mama told me I was laid as an egg stuck to the bottom of a milkweed leaf. I was just a little white egg stuck to a milkweed leaf, which was my first stage. I emerged into a caterpillar from my egg after a while. Inside my egg, I was growing into a caterpillar. I pushed my way out of the egg. I started eating, eating and eating. I just couldn't help myself. I was so hungry for those yummy milkweed leaves. Oh dear, I had a problem though, my skin became too small, well actually my body became too big for my skin. You see all that eating and eating turned me into a bigger plumped caterpillar, so I shed my skin. I wiggled right out of my old skin and grew a new skin that better accommodated my larger body. Cool! Right? I started experiencing what is called moulting. While I was still in stage two, the larval stage (caterpillar), being a caterpillar and eating like crazy, I moulted four or five times. Not too sure though, I guess it was four times. I looked so good. Just when I thought I couldn't look any more terrific, I ate enough milkweed leaves and things started to change for me. Remember metamorphosis? Something came over me. I turned upside down within it and was dangling upside down from the leaves. I wrapped myself in a blanket called Chrysalis. This is a stage called the pupa stage (3rd stage). The outside of my Chrysalis starts off as a green colour. Kind of like a wrapped-up leaf. Inside, though, I was transforming my ugly-looking caterpillar body into a stunning colourful butterfly. It's like a science magic, but it's actually metamorphosis. So, I had been hanging up there in my Chrysalis for about two weeks and growing wings, getting prettied up for my big day of showing forth my beauty. Just like my body, my Chrysalis was also changing. Remember, it used to look like a wrapped up green leaf. Well, as we get closer to my big day, my Chrysalis became transparent. Everybody out there could see through my Chrysalis and catch a glimpse of what is happening to me on the inside from the outside. I was undergoing some changes. Finally, it was my big day; I burst out of my Chrysalis. It splits open, which marks the last stage of my life circle. I had piled up plans for that day, but first I had to get myself organised. My head, abdomen, and legs came out of my Chrysalis first. And my wings were wet and not working yet, but my abdomen was swollen with lots of fluid. I pumped the fluid into my wings and they started expanding and stretching out. So, I sat quietly on a branch, resting and waiting for my wings to dry. I was exhausted. Metamorphosis is not an easy process I must confess, but it's worth doing. When my wings got dried and hard, I knew I was ready to fly. In no time, I was out to town, checking out the pretty flowers and sipping nectars. This is the life I have been waiting for. I love this stage four. It's full of excitement, fulfilment, achievements, adventures and glamour. So now, you know all about how I became a butterfly starting with my cute little egg stuck on a milkweed leaf to an ugly caterpillar, pupa and finally to the new me you can see now. My mum was so proud of me! You too can do this. You have what it takes on your inside. Go for it and be patient with the process.

Caterpillar: Thank you very much. I can't wait to eat up and undergo this rigorous process. Though it takes time, I will wait for it. My outward change will come, my beauty will emerge for all to see as well.

Adult Butterfly: Your welcome.

Chapter 4

RENEWING YOUR MIND WITH THE WORD OF GRACE

The Word of Grace is your tool for renewal. You need to continuously renew your mind with the Word of Grace. It's important you get your thoughts right by setting your mind on the things of God. You may wonder why good people sin, backslide, or experience poverty. Some fail in marriage, life and destiny, or are faced with various addictions and habits. All these are because of the absence of the renewal of the mind. They are born-again Christians, but they still experience what the world experiences. They still find themselves stuck in some challenges. This is not because there is no grace to be victorious, but they have not been renewed to it through the Word. The power of the Christian life is released when you are renewed in the spirit of your mind to what grace has done for you. This power flows through our minds into our lives as we commit to mind renewal. It does not flow from your mind; it flows through your mind. Grace flows through your mind to all avenues of your life. Mind renewal is not a function of your intellectuality, theology, nor knowing facts about the Bible. It is about the reconstruction of your mind to align with the will of God and setting your mind on God to experience His power, His blessings and His life in all areas of your life. When you get born-again, your spirit (the real you) is completely saved, but your mind, will and emotion may fight the spirit. At new birth, you have a new spirit, but an unrenewed mind. You must continually renew your mind. There was a way you used to think, and a way you used to act before you got born-again. We have been told to repent, to change our ways but we are supposed to change our thoughts as well. Let's forsake our old ways and old thoughts; not just forsake the old lifestyle but also forsake the old thought patterns. We have neglected a very powerful part of our makeup that regulates other things around us. What we do has its origin from what goes on in our minds. Your actions have a direct correlation with your thoughts. Your mind is like the womb of your life. What you nurture, nourish and cultivate in your mind, you give birth to in your life. Everything around your life is regulated by what goes on in your mind. What you give birth to is what your mind has nurtured over time. If you don't like the result you are seeing, change the way you think about that issue. Renewing your mind is a process of change every believer must adopt. We are in an age where people desire a sudden change of story, easy fixes and make-it-in-a-day prosperity schemes. We live in a microwave world, we just want it quickly but are never ready to undergo the process of change. Renewing your mind is like reformatting your mind and reinstalling a new software of the Word of Grace; putting away the old and putting in the new. There is a new reality that grace brings to you; you cannot maximise it if you are not renewed to it. Without a paradigm shift from your old thought patterns, you will live a life parallel to your new realities in Christ. The enemy of the new is the old. What was your old perspective about prosperity? What was your old perspective about righteousness? What was your old perspective about divine health? What was your old perspective about God's love for you? How did you see God before you became born-again? Did you see Him as mean? What was your perspective about God's blessings? All these and more are what you should look into because if you have a negative perspective, it will be impossible to experience the goodness of God in its totality. Until you renew your mind, it can take you back to your old experiences even if you are born-again. Grace does not breed irresponsible believers; grace brings responsibility. If you are in for real, be ready to work to renew your mind to enjoy the abundant grace for real. There is no overnight success with grace; it's a process of change to accept what Jesus has done for you that guarantees your success. Let's explore the content of grace and renew our minds to it. Your life will only be transformed when your mind is renewed.

> *Beloved, I pray that you may prosper in all things*
> *and be in health, just as your soul prospers.*
> III JOHN 1:2

Notice that the prosperity of your soul is equated to your all-around prosperity. Your prosperity, divine health, dominion, and establishment in life are directly correlated to the prosperity of your mind. Above all things God wants you to prosper, He wants you to be in health, but the prosperity of your soul must match. It must be equal; your mind must be renewed to the abundant life grace has for you. You cannot enjoy grace beyond the level to which your mind is renewed to it. Whatever you have aligned your mind with is what you are permitted to get. A sound mind will produce a sound living. If you think parallel to God's will for healing, you can't get healed. If you think parallel to God's will for prosperity, you can't prosper. If you think parallel to God's will for breakthrough, you can't attain one. The more you allow your soul (mind) to prosper, the more prosperous your life becomes. God wills good for you, but your mind has to be renewed for you to experience it. We are all in different phases of renewing our minds. The level of our mind renewal determines what we can enjoy from God's provisions.

> *I beseech you therefore, brethren, by the mercies of God,*
> *that ye present your bodies a living sacrifice, holy, acceptable unto*
> *God, which is your reasonable service. And be not conformed to this*
> *world: but be ye transformed by the renewing of your mind,*
> *that ye may prove what is that good, and acceptable,*
> *and perfect, will of God.*
> ROMANS 12:1-2

The transforming of your life works hand in hand with the renewing of your mind. When you got born-again God did not remove your mind. He wants you to renew it and use it to transform your life. It is meant for you to think in line with God's will for you, not in opposition to God's will. In Romans 12:1-2, your spirit was not mentioned because you have a new spirit, the only concern was your body and your mind.

Paul, a great Apostle writing to born-again, spirit-filled Christians, admonished them not to be conformed to the world, but to be transformed by the renewing of their minds. He implied that you can be born-again and still be dragged to act like the world. You can't act like the world and expect to have victory in the Kingdom of God. Your mind can conform to the world system if not renewed. To be conformed is to be shaped like or to look like the world. Sometimes you are unable to differentiate between a believer and someone in the world. This is because some believers still tend to act and look like the world. You are supposed to present your body as a living sacrifice, holy, acceptable unto God and renew your mind to experience change. Romans 12:2 uses the word *prove*, meaning to experience, to demonstrate, and to manifest. You cannot demonstrate what is the good, acceptable and perfect will of God if your mind is not renewed to the things of God, to the Kingdom of God and the ways of God. God wills good for you, but you may not experience all that good if you are not willing to change your mind and to align your mind to agree with God. God wills for you to be healed, but you are not going to walk in divine health if you don't align your thought with God and your philosophy with God. You need to abandon your philosophies and perspectives concerning your old thought patterns. You should think differently than the world thinks, you should talk differently than the world talks and you should act differently than the world acts. Your mind is the bridge through which God's goodness (grace) is shipped to your life.

BE TRANSFORMED

The word *transform* is a Greek word *metamorphoo* meaning to radically change the structure of. It emphasises a total change from inside out. It's also a compound verb comprised of meta (implying change) and morphe, meaning form; having to do with the special or characteristic form or feature of a person or thing. The English word *metamorphosis* comes from this word. When you got born-again, a drastic change occurred in your spirit. You were totally changed and received a new spirit. The old was taken away. Inherent in your spirit was the very life of God. You were given things that pertained to life and godliness in your spirit. Your spirit was made perfect, but your body and mind are yet perfect. Transformation needs to happen. Without transformation, you will have all it will take to excel in this life only in your spirit. Grace has been given and deposited in your spirit (Philemon 1:25). Each one of us has a measure of grace. You carry God's life on your inside. This life has to be expressed on the outside. Let's take for instance a tadpole turning into a frog and a caterpillar turning into a butterfly. The radical change that occurs in turning the tadpole to a frog is called metamorphosis, also known as transformation. Notice that all the features it displayed as a frog are what it had on the inside as a tadpole. These features are not something that comes externally; they evolve internally. It's an inside-out process. Likewise, when you get born-again, you don't stop there. You have to undergo a process of change to enjoy the Christian life. It's a process that brings out your true nature in Christ to be evident on the outside. In your spirit, you have been made righteous by grace, blessed, healed, made prosperous, and given the rivers of living water that have to flow from inside out (the Holy Spirit) when you got baptised in the Holy Ghost. Let your life take the form of the life that Christ has given unto you by salvation. You have so much treasure on your inside; you have to draw it out by faith through renewing your mind with the Word of Grace, so that you will experience metamorphosis into what you have seen in the Word of Grace concerning your inner content. No matter how much you look outwardly now, it has nothing to do with how much deposit is inside you. Christ in you is the hope of glory (Colossians 1:27). You have received everything in your spirit man. Take a look at the caterpillar that turns radically into a butterfly. A beautiful butterfly evolves from an ugly-looking caterpillar that was living a low life. The caterpillar drastically changes from living a low life to high life. It flies gloriously now! It could fly in its early stage as a caterpillar, but it couldn't prove it. It's not aware of what it's made of. It could not demonstrate it. That's the change every Christian should experience. It's a change coming from the inside, you have been changed already by redemption, but you just have to be renewed to this change to see on the outside that beautiful part of you, that glamorous part that is already in you. You are only going to draw it out. It's exceptionally a grace work in you. Grace made it happen. You need that same grace to experience the practical manifestation in your life. Align yourself with the grace of God and see your life emerge as an expression of grace. From that point on, you can see that you are not a sinner, even if you sometimes sin. You are not poor even if you don't have money in your pocket now. You are not sick even if you look or feel sick. Look into the Word of Grace and see what grace has made of you, then start appropriating it to your life through mind renewal and faith. Then you can live totally above sin, knowing that by grace you have been given dominion over sin, so that sin shall not have dominion over you. You will realise that you are empowered by grace for wealth, you just have to respond by faith to that reality. You will realise how healed you are and that it would be an illegality for you to experience any form of sickness and disease. Please note that it's a process, you don't get renewed in one day. Mind renewal is totally a work of grace, it's not memorising Scriptures or an intellectual show of how many Scriptures you can quote. It's allowing the Holy Spirit to teach you, and eradicating every form of old philosophy you used to have in your mind. You need to totally put away your old perspective and yield yourself to the Holy Spirit to open you up to grace.

> *But we all, with open face beholding as in a glass the glory of the Lord, are changed into the same image from glory to glory, even as by the Spirit of the Lord.*
> 2 CORINTHIANS 3:18

To change means to be transformed, to metamorphose. You are changed into the same image. Conforming to Christ is done with the help of the Holy Spirit. You see, if you try to engage in it in the energy of the flesh, you will struggle. Allow grace to have its free course in your life. Let the Holy Spirit take charge, stop thinking you know something when it comes to studying. Submit yourself to the teaching ministry the Holy Ghost. The reflection of your true self in Christ is revealed and made manifest for all to see when you undergo the process of renewing your mind through the Word of Grace.

BE NOT CONFORMED

Be not conformed to this world. Don't allow yourself to be dragged into doing what the world does. Don't adjust to the world system. Don't be on the fence. If you are born-again, engage in renewing your mind to behave as born-again. Don't lose your identity in Christ to conform to the world. There are a lot of people out there who want to experience salvation, they don't enjoy what they are doing. The devil has enslaved them. They don't know how to get out. You are supposed to show forth the beauty of what it means to be born-again. You are supposed to be a role model so they can admire you and want what you have. Don't stoop low to do what they do. Be true to who you have become in Christ. You are born-again. Why not fully stand for what you believe and apply the Biblical principles to enjoy the beautiful things God has deposited in you in Christ Jesus? You will not be able to express the life of God to the fullest if you conform to this world. Be conformed to the image of Christ. He is your standard, and you are to show the world the standard.

> *For whom he did foreknow, he also did predestinate*
> *to be conformed to the image of his Son, that he might be the*
> *firstborn among many brethren.*
> ROMANS 8:29

God knew you before you were born. He had your future planned already before you came. He had a complete knowledge of you beforehand. One of the fundamental things He had in His plan was to have you conformed to the image of His Son Jesus Christ and for you to be exactly like Him. Since the day Adam failed, God had a plan, but waited until it was time for Christ to come to earth for it to be executed. Christ is now living in you. You have the life of Christ in you. Christ in you is the hope of glory. You still have the responsibility to conform to Christ. Look like Him in all your dispositions. Let His life be expressed in your life. As He is, so are you. You are not to be different from Him. Your transformation process determines your conformation. When your mind is renewed, then you will experience transformation, and when this happen, you won't succumb to the things of this world any longer. You will just naturally conform to the image of Jesus Christ.

PROVE

The Word *prove* in Scripture means to experience, to demonstrate and to manifest. You can't prove or demonstrate the good, acceptable and perfect will of God if you refuse to renew your mind. No matter how much God cares and wants you to prosper and enjoy life, He will never take responsibility for things you are meant to do to align yourself for the blessings He has released. Manifestation is your responsibility; it can only happen when you are fully aligned with God's will for your life. When your mind is renewed, you think the way God thinks, you see the way God sees, you talk the way God talks and you automatically start manifesting everything God desires in your life.

> *For the earnest expectation of the creature waiteth for the manifestation of the sons of God.*
> ROMANS 8:19

The world is waiting for your manifestation. The sons of God have to prove the good, acceptable and perfect will of God. We need to live it out. Every good thing is to be displayed from our lives, everything that is acceptable to God, not working contrary to God but working in alignment with God knowing the perfect will of God for your life and living it. Your outward man should reflect that you know God's perfect will for your promotion, your establishment, for your breakthrough, your blessings, and your health. The world is waiting to see the believer display God, and grace is available for everyone to manifest. The proportion to which you renew your mind determines your level of manifestation.

FORSAKING YOUR WAYS AND YOUR THOUGHTS

Our ways and our thoughts before we came to know Christ must be forsaken. We really need to forsake our thoughts. Many times, we are taught to forsake our ways, in others words, to repent, or change your ways. We may have changed our ways, but may still experience some challenges and mess, not knowing that it's not your ways only that are messing your life up but also your thoughts. Until your thought is totally forsaken, no matter how many times you have repented, you will still find yourself doing some things you don't like to do if your thoughts are not addressed. You need to get rid of your old thought patterns and fill them with new thoughts of the Word of God. The Word of God is God's ways, the Word of God is God's thoughts. We struggle with God's ways and thoughts because we refuse to forsake our ways and thoughts. Put away your old perspectives about things and seek God's perspectives. Clean your mind with the Word of Grace. Outside of the spiritual change that took place in your life when you got born-again, nothing truly changes physically until your mind changes. Your blessings, prosperity, progress, breakthrough, divine health, and marital bliss are all hinged on changing the way you think. It's not just the changing of your ways that will make you live a new life in abundance but changing your thoughts as well. You can't experience what God has done if your mind is not in union with it. You have to do this yourself and yield to the Holy Spirit to help you as you engage in mind renewal. You have to get into the Word and allow the Holy Spirit to reconstruct your mind as you study. Forsake your opinion for God's opinion. Forsake your mind for God's mind. Release your mind to be worked on because there is a philosophy regarding virtually every matter and you were once in the world. You carry along those thoughts with you when you are in Christ now. There is an attitude of your mind that has to be dealt with.

Let the wicked forsake his way, and the unrighteous man his thoughts: and let him return unto the Lord, and he will have mercy upon him; and to our God, for he will abundantly pardon. For my thoughts are not your thoughts, neither are your ways my ways, saith the Lord. For as the heavens are higher than the earth, so are my ways higher than your ways, and my thoughts than your thoughts.
ISAIAH 55:7-9

What we think most times is in parallel to what God thinks, making it difficult to achieve results. Let's put down what we know. It's pride to have your opinion after giving your life to Christ. You don't own that life anymore. It's not yours, and you can't live it on your own terms. You can never become all He has ordained you to be if you don't submit your thoughts to His thoughts. Your mind has to agree with God's ways and thoughts.

That ye put off concerning the former conversation the old man, which is corrupt according to the deceitful lusts; And be renewed in the spirit of your mind; And that ye put on the new man, which after God is created in righteousness and true holiness.
EPHESIANS 4:22-24

You have a new man on the inside of you, which is Christ in union with your spirit. He is righteous and truly holy so also are you. You can't live this Christ life in your own strength and power. It is only possible when you put away your old man. Allow your mind to be reconstructed to take the right shape. You have to be renewed in the spirit of your mind to live this Christian life.

SETTING YOUR MIND ABOVE

*If ye then be risen with Christ, seek those things which are above, where Christ sitteth on the right hand of God.
Set your affection on things above, not on things on the earth.*
COLOSSIANS 3:1-2

Set your affection on things above, not on things on the earth. If you be risen with Christ, you are to seek things above. If you are born-again, you are risen with Christ. Now that you have a new life, you need to set your affection on Him. Your affection which is from your mind, will, and emotion, should be to God. Set your mind on God. Yield your mind to God, and He will reconstruct your mind. It's your responsibility to give Him your mind; He will supernaturally renew your mind. It's all grace work. You can't do it in the energy of the flesh. Surrender your mind to Him; He will do the renewal.

> *Lie not one to another, seeing that ye have put off the old man with his deeds; And have put on the new man, which is renewed in knowledge after the image of him that created him:*
> COLOSSIANS 3:9-10

After putting off the old man, you have to keep renewing your mind in this new man to conform to the image of Jesus that created the new you. Otherwise, you will act or conform to the world pattern because your mind can drag you back to your past if you allow it. The ball is in your court. Your mind needs to be renewed to be like Christ. As He is, so are you now, but that's in your spirit. If you want to be exactly like Him in the physical and in all spheres of life, then set your mind on Him. That's the key to a victorious and fulfilling life.

> *Thou wilt keep him in perfect peace, whose mind is stayed on thee: because he trusteth in thee.*
> ISAIAH 26:3

Your mind has to stay on the Lord. You have to allow Him to work on your mind. That's what guarantees perfect peace.

> *Finally, brethren, whatsoever things are true, whatsoever things are honest, whatsoever things are just, whatsoever things are pure, whatsoever things are lovely, whatsoever things are of good report; if there be any virtue, and if there be any praise, think on these things.*
> PHILIPPIANS 4:8

You can see clearly from this Scripture what things to think on. Set your mind on these things and you will be amazed at how God will supernaturally renew your mind. When you do this, God takes away those wrong attitudes and puts in the right attitude, the right mindset. It's a grace work; your role is to submit to the work of grace, while the Holy Spirit does the part of the supernatural transformation. Eventually, you manifest the changes on the outside. That is the reason sometimes you can't explain what has happened to you over time when you truly give yourself to the Word of Grace and allow the Holy Spirit to teach you. Drastic changes just take place like the caterpillar turning into a beautiful butterfly. God from within works on you and brings out His qualities on the outside. It's God at work in you both to will and to do of His good pleasure. Allow Him.

MEDITATE ON THE WORD OF GOD

One of the ways to set your affection on God is through meditation. Meditate on the things of God. The love of God, the Kingdom of God, the ways of God and the thoughts of God.

TAKE AWAY DECLARATIONS

I have the mind of Christ in me. My mind is renewed with the Word of Grace.

I yield my mind to be renewed by the Word of Grace through the power of the Holy Spirit.

I forsake my old thoughts and opinions. I rely on what God's word has said concerning me.

I live by the grace of God; I lean not on my own understanding.

I meditate on things that are true, honest, just, pure, lovely and of good report (Philippians 4:8).

I am transformed as I engage in mind renewal in Jesus name (Romans 12:2).

I refuse to live a low life when I am destined for a high life in Christ. As I renew my mind, I translate into practical manifestation all the good and beautiful things Christ has done in me to be seen on the outside.

I experience prosperity and live in health as I renew my mind with the Word of Grace (III John 1:2).

I align myself by faith with all the good things that God has done in me through Christ Jesus as I renew my mind (Philemon 1:6).

PRE-CHAPTER POEM

UNMERITED FAVOUR

The depth of His love, we cannot comprehend. It surpasses human comprehension. He so loved us and gave His life for us. We did not deserve it, but He decided to do it anyway. We couldn't earn it by our works of righteousness. He went all the way to lay down His life on the cross for us even while we were crossed with Him. It was not an easy task, but it was worth doing for the sake of the love He has for us. What an unmerited favour. This is huge, that sweet moment when love and grace blend to put an end to our struggles. We thought that was all and celebrated this amazing grace that brought salvation. We found out that this favour keeps speaking in every aspect of our lives. We thought this undeserved favour was just for our salvation, never knew it was a lifelong favour. We never knew it was meant for our continuous advancement in life. When we were lost in the crowd, that searchlight of His grace searched for us and found us. When we lost our way, we found a new way of living in His grace. When we were rejected, His favour granted us unusual acceptability. His favour made a way for us where there seemed to be no way. We're excelling by His supernatural favour. It's all we have. We can't pay for it. It has set us on pedestals that our human legs couldn't climb on their own. It's not our smartness, cleverness, hard work or wisdom, but His undeniable underserved favour at work in our lives.

Chapter 5
THE UNMERITED FAVOUR DIMENSION OF GRACE

Unmerited favour is an integral part of God's grace. It's an accompanist of grace. Where there is grace, there is favour associated with it. A favour you do not deserve. We have established that grace is far more than unmerited favour. Grace is a huge package that has diverse by-products. It is God's Reliable Abundance by Christ's Effort. Grace is more than just a concept; it's the power of God at work in your life. It is God's ability in humanity to act supernaturally in the natural; God's empowerment in your life to withstand sin, make wealth, be blessed and be a blessing to others. It is your advantage for a successful life on earth.

> *But God commendeth his love toward us, in that, while we were yet sinners, Christ died for us. For if, when we were enemies, we were reconciled to God by the death of his Son, much more, being reconciled, we shall be saved by his life.*
> ROMANS 5:8 & 10

The gift of grace was a gift of love given to us who did not deserve to be loved. We were God's enemies but still He lavished his grace on us. We were against Him even before He sent His Son to die for us. We have all sinned and come short of His glory (Romans 3:23). We couldn't meet His perfect standard. We wronged Him; we kicked against Him. We were against love instead of loving Him. Even while we were alienated from Him, He was still loving us and gave us the most expensive gift ever. We were reconciled back to God while we were enemies to Him. Have you ever imagined loving your enemies? That's what God did for you and me by sending Christ to us.

> *For by grace are ye saved through faith; and that not of yourselves: it is the gift of God: Not of works, lest any man should boast.*
> EPHESIANS 2:8-9

Grace is an expression of God's goodness towards undeserving people. Grace saves us. Your salvation is a gift of grace. You could not have walked into it by your works. Grace favoured you. You did not work for it. You did not earn it by your works. He worked all things for you to enjoy. That's why it is unmerited favour, something you received without merit. No work on your end, you are just enjoying the privileges of the work done by Jesus Christ. All you have enjoyed and all you will ever enjoy are wrapped up in God's grace. Salvation and its fringe benefits came by unmerited favour. They are the unearned release of God's goodness towards those who believe. We did not deserve righteousness, justification, blessings, favour, healing, or breakthrough. We deserved punishment for our actions, but mercy said, "NO!" to us from receiving the penalties for what we had done, and grace said, "YES!" to us receiving what we did nothing to earn. We were doomed for condemnation, but grace released justification and rescued us from condemnation and guilt. You were a candidate for hell; you became a candidate for heaven. You did not deserve it, but He gave it to you anyway. You were a candidate for sickness, disease, poverty, reproach and failure, but grace made you a candidate for divine health, divine wealth, glory, success and all-around riches. Unmerited favour is your supernatural advantage to living a super-successful life. It all started with you receiving what you did not work for. How then do you think you can maintain it with your struggles or works? What you need is faith and total alignment with what has been accomplished for you by Christ Jesus. Unmerited favour is not just a favour you receive at salvation; it is a favour that keeps giving. You keep having favour with God and man. You became a candidate for this continuous favour by salvation. You need to understand this and keep growing in it.

> *He that spared not his own Son, but delivered him up for us all, how shall he not with him also freely give us all things?*
> ROMANS 8:32

God gave His Son as undeserved favour that was birthed by love. That same favour is still at work to give to us all things to freely enjoy. God is interested in favouring you. God wants to favour you on every side. If you have never believed in favour, it's time to have a paradigm shift about it. You have to be favour-conscious. If you are the type that believes in luck, it is time to change your perspective. In the Kingdom of God there is no such thing as luck. What happens around you and in you are the result of grace. When you refuse to acknowledge that you are being favoured and do not trust God for more favour, you are limited. What you don't celebrate cannot appreciate. You need favour with God and with man to excel in this life. I believe in favour, I have enjoyed supernatural favour, and I am still growing in it. You need favour with your boss, you need favour in your school, you need favour at your workplace, you need favour in your business, you need favour with your spouse and children, you need favour with everyone around you, you need favour for that job interview, you need favour for a good grade in that course even if you have read. You don't only run to God for favour when you feel inadequate or unqualified. You should learn to live a life of favour. Whether you are well prepared or qualified for that interview, you still need to yield yourself to God's favour. That's how favour can be multiplied in your life. God always favours the course of the humble. He wants people who can depend on Him for everything. He wants to be your source of supply. He personally wants to favour you; He wants the glory to come back to Him. His favour adds flavour to your labour. It gives beauty to your labour and converts your errors to honour. God's favour opens supernatural provision for you. It guarantees your promotion. As a grace carrier, you are accompanied by favour everywhere you go. Let's quickly define favour for better understanding. When you understand favour, you will be able to stand under the influence of favour at any time, any day and anywhere. Then you can also recognise favor when you see it and celebrate it.

What is favour? Favour is the divine attraction of God towards you that unleashes His influence through you so that people will supernaturally like you, trust you and to be benevolent to you. God's favour is an attraction that draws the attention of people to you, to like you and to be benevolent to you. People supernaturally like you without knowing why. It is called favour. It is the cure to rejection. It is God's likability upon your life that causes people to like you without a reason. Favour is an irresistible charisma of Christ that wraps up a believer to be influential in His assignment. It takes favour to carry out the assignment God has assigned you to do. You can't have impact without favour. There is an anointing that emanates from you that makes you preferred and favourable. Even Jesus operated in this favour. As a man, you need favour. You should expect favour always. The favour of God can make a way for you when you can't make any on your own. God's favour is His goodwill to mankind, His loving-kindness upon your life. Favour will release great blessings, including prosperity, health, opportunity and supernatural advancement. Nothing in life can hold you down when you have God's favour and blessing upon your life. The favour of God is also God's supernatural avenue through you to promote the course of the Kingdom. God wants to promote the kingdom course by favouring you and me. As we progress we will discuss more on why God favours you, and examine Biblical examples of those who enjoyed God's favour. Even Jesus, who was not only God made flesh, but also fully a man as well needed to increase in favour also. Jesus did not come to live a life that is impossible for us to live. He came to teach us how to live life. The life of Jesus is our possibility on earth. He is our pattern for living, our standard. He is the first begotten of a new race, which is the grace race. He is the firstborn amongst many brethren where we belong. He showed us the pattern of living and how to live as well. We are all products of this grace. Express grace and grow in every facet of it as depicted by Jesus Christ.

> *And Jesus increased in wisdom and stature,*
> *and in favour with God and man.*
> LUKE 2:52

Jesus increased in wisdom and maturity, the word *stature* here means *maturity*. He also increased in favour with God and man. We are also supposed to increase in wisdom, stature and in favour with God and man. Irrespective of who you are, you need favour with God and everyone around you. You don't have to negotiate for favour; you don't have to lobby for it, you don't need to manipulate people to get it, you don't have to trick anybody. God is the giver of favour; you just have to yield yourself by faith to be favoured. God wills for us to increase in favour.

Let's have a quick look at some Biblical accounts of people that experienced divine favour.

> *And I will give this people favour in the sight of the Egyptians: and it shall come to pass, that, when ye go, ye shall not go empty.*
> *[22] But every woman shall borrow of her neighbour, and of her that sojourneth in her house, jewels of silver, and jewels of gold, and raiment: and ye shall put them upon your sons, and upon your daughters; and ye shall spoil the Egyptians.*
> EXODUS 3:21-22

The children of Israel were in bondage in a strange land, Egypt. They were under oppressions and afflictions for over four hundred years. God saw their afflictions and sent Moses to be their deliverer. It came to pass on this faithful day that God said He wanted them to find favour in the sight of their haters. He desired to favour them by the same people that had been afflicting them. Favour can make your enemies give all they have to be a blessing to you. It is an irresistible power of God upon your life that makes people like you even when you seem unlikable. God guaranteed that the Hebrews did not go empty, He caused them to experience supernatural favour. Favour located the Israelites and they made away with all the valuables of the Egyptians. They stripped the

Egyptians of their possessions. They spoiled the Egyptians; nothing was left behind. This would not have happened on a normal day. It only happened on a platform of favour. When favour speaks for you, protocols are suspended. Favour violates the norm for the abnormal to take place. Abnormal here implies the supernatural. We are in a most profound season in the body of Christ. It's a prophetic season and one of the things that characterises this season amongst others is the supernatural transfer of wealth from the heathen to the Christian for the promotion of kingdom course. This does not restrict your favour to unbelievers only. It simply means that you are going to have supernatural favour from both the household of faith and from those who have refused to join the fold. Those are the unbelievers. The church will be a great attraction to all. The Lord is decking his church with beauty. In these last days, there is a transference of the wealth of the world to the Church. We need supernatural favour to get the Gospel out. It requires finances to get the work of the kingdom done, but favour is what gets the job done. Favour is what makes people want to release what they have to promote the propagation of the Gospel.

> *Ask of me, and I shall give thee the heathen for thine inheritance, and the uttermost parts of the earth for thy possession.*
> PSALM 2:8

This is what the Lord means in the above Scripture: He only wants you to ask in faith and believe for His favour. What you don't expect, you cannot experience. You need to consciously expect to be favoured. You don't have to struggle for it. It's the Lord's work to favour you.

> *A good man leaveth an inheritance to his children's children: and the wealth of the sinner is laid up for the just.*
> PROVERBS 13:22

We are living in the era of wealth transfer. The wealth of sinners (the ungodly) is laid up for the just. It does not wait for you to get to heaven. It is your reality on earth, happening to you now by grace. The just are wealthy people. You are the just by new birth. You have been made the righteousness of God in Christ Jesus. This wealth is for the body of Christ, and it is for the promotion of the Kingdom of God. The ungodly laboured for you. You entered into their labour by favour. In other words, you are enjoying or reaping from another's labour. It's called favour to receive what you did not work for. That's how this Christian race started. You received Jesus Christ without paying any acceptance fees. There was no cost to it. You did not have to work for it. You earned approval by unmerited favour. Your acceptance fee was your faith. God gave us His Dear Son on the platform of undeserved favour, and with it, He also unleashed divine favour upon us to excel in all our endeavours.

And herein is that saying true, One soweth, and another reapeth. I sent you to reap that whereon ye bestowed no labour: other men laboured, and ye are entered into their labours.
JOHN 4:37-38

The favour God wants you to enjoy is the one that positions you for reaping. You don't have to labour to be favoured; others laboured, and you are entered into their labour. That's the work of favour in your life. That's what Jesus expects you to enjoy. If your shifts or hours of labour is what you depend on, you have not started putting the favour of God to work in your life. God wants to bless you beyond your earnings, beyond your work. He wants you to enjoy favour from multiple channels, not only from the work of your hand. He wants you to reap where you did not bestow labour. That's the work of grace. Jesus did all the work needed to be done on the cross and called you to believe and receive all the benefits. You are to continue in this favour with God and man receiving by faith for work you did not perform. Expect to be favoured.

So it came to pass, when the king's commandment and his decree was heard, and when many maidens were gathered together unto Shushan the palace, to the custody of Hegai, that Esther was brought also unto the king's house, to the custody of Hegai, keeper of the women. And the maiden pleased him, and she obtained kindness

> *of him; and he speedily gave her her things for purification, with such things as belonged to her, and seven maidens, which were meet to be given her, out of the king's house: and he preferred her and her maids unto the best place of the house of the women.*
> ESTHER 2:8-9

> *Now when the turn of Esther, the daughter of Abihail the uncle of Mordecai, who had taken her for his daughter, was come to go in unto the king, she required nothing but what Hegai the king's chamberlain, the keeper of the women, appointed. And Esther obtained favour in the sight of all them that looked upon her.*
> ESTHER 2:15

Let's look at what God's favour did in Esther's life and how we should expect to be favoured in everything we do. The rise of an unknown Jewish girl to become queen of a mighty empire depicts favour. Favour was all over her. It was a supernatural attraction of God upon her that drew attention to her. As soon as she entered the king's house, in the custody of Hegai the keeper of the women, favour began to emanate from her. She pleased Hegai at her arrival. She did not lobby for it. Immediately she was given preferential treatment and obtained kindness in his sight. She was given all she needed for purification, including seven maidens out of the king's house. She was preferred more than other virgin maidens. She and her maids were given the best place to stay in the house of the women. Only the best is good enough for the favoured. Favour is what distinguishes you from others. It is what makes your case different whenever you appear. You outshine your competitors by virtue of the favour of God upon your life. She was not the most beautiful, but the favour of God in her made her beauty draw attention. Favour makes you noticeable. When favour is on you, you can't hide in the crowd because favour will find you out. It will single you out for honour. When her turn in the beauty pageant came, she obtained favour in the sight of all them that looked upon her. She was not the only participant, but she was the only one that was noticed. The Bible did not say, "Behold the most beautiful amongst the virgin maidens."

No, she was the most favoured. Her true beauty was the favour of God. Everyone looked at her and preferred her. Favour easily won the contest for beauty. This is what we should crave to experience; it is God's favour that turns things around for your good.

> *And the king loved Esther above all the women,*
> *and she obtained grace and favour in his sight more than all the*
> *virgins; so that he set the royal crown upon her head,*
> *and made her queen instead of Vashti.*
> ESTHER 2:17

The king loved Esther above all the women, and she obtained grace and favour in his sight more than all the virgins. Favour is your distinguisher. If you want to be distinguished, prefer favour and always expect favour. Favour and grace go hand in hand. It's an accompanist of grace. Where you see grace, you see favour. Favour made her case to be different; the king saw her differently compared to other. She was likeable and adorable because of favour. God wants to give you favour both with unbelievers and believers. Notice that this was an ungodly king who favoured Esther, who was a child of God. She had favour with ungodly people in a strange land. Your enthronement is in you having favour with God and man. It's not the nature of the country that determines your enthronement; it's the nature of the God you carry that favours you for enthronement in a foreign country. He wants you to experience favour with the world at large. King Ahasuerus appointed Esther to replace Queen Vashti. For Kingdom purposes, God will displace and replace where necessary. What happened to Vashti was never done in the law before, but it happened so that a child of God could take her place. God wanted Esther to be in the place of influence to rescue her people, the Jews in the land. There are many opportunities out there for the Esthers of this generation to promote the kingdom course in government, businesses, education, and other public arenas. It will only happen by favour. God left us here in this world to make a difference. He wants to go ahead of us to make the crooked way straight by favour. You can't make a difference in your world without having favour in your assignment.

> *And it was so, when the king saw Esther the queen standing in the court, that she obtained favour in his sight: and the king held out to Esther the golden sceptre that was in his hand. So Esther drew near, and touched the top of the sceptre. Then said the king unto her, What wilt thou, queen Esther? and what is thy request? it shall be even given thee to the half of the kingdom.*
> ESTHER 5:2-3

Haman had plotted to slay all the Jews in the land because Mordecai refused to bow to him at the gate. Then Mordecai told his cousin Esther about all that was before her people and admonished her to speak to the king. The decree had been made, and it was sealed with the king's ring just awaiting execution. Esther was afraid, but Mordecai asked her if this was purpose she was sent "for such a time as this?" (Esther 4:14). In other words, that was the reason God gave her such favour. Favour is not for selfish gain, but kingdom purpose. Esther requested the Jews fast and pray for three days because it was forbidden by law for anyone to go into the king's inner court uninvited. Anybody that went in uninvited could be slain unless the king held out his golden sceptre. If he did, the person could live. Peradventure he didn't, that person would die.

Esther knew the rules and with courage in her heart, she determined that if she must die, then she would die. She was willing to take the risk. When she did, she obtained favour. The king held out the golden sceptre and welcomed her into his inner chamber. That meant the law was suspended. Protocols were broken. She was able to get through and make her request. The king asked Esther what her request was, and was willing to give her anything, even up to half the kingdom! Without favour, she would have been killed. The bottom line is that she was given audience in a daring situation and her request was granted. The Jews were delivered from their enemies, and Haman took the place of the proposed death of Mordecai. I see God's favour giving you audience before kings. Favour will make the seemingly impossible situation possible for you in Jesus name. Wherever the law has placed a restriction, God's supernatural favour will suspend restrictions and grant you supernatural access to your provisions and desires in Jesus name!

> *But Daniel purposed in his heart that he would not defile himself with the portion of the king's meat, nor with the wine which he drank: therefore he requested of the prince o f the eunuchs that he might not defile himself. Now God had brought Daniel into favour and tender love with the prince of the eunuchs.*
> DANIEL 1:8-9

Daniel purposed in his heart that he would not defile himself with the king's meat, nor with the king's wine. Therefore, he made a request of the prince of the eunuchs of what he and his friends would like to eat. In Daniel's culture, there are certain things that should not be eaten, and he noticed them in the king's meat. He decided not to eat. The king had made arrangement for all the teenagers to be fed with food from the king's table. In Babylonian culture, there are certain beliefs that when you partake of certain food, you will be well nourished and possess wisdom, you will be smart. The Hebrew youths were in training. God gave Daniel favour with the prince of the eunuchs so that they were given what they desired to eat instead of what the king sanctioned for them to eat. It was not the norm, but God's favour made it possible. If you read other verses of chapter one of Daniel, you will realise that the prince of the eunuch was concerned and did not want to be questioned for not feeding Daniel and his friends well. As God would have it, they appeared more fair and healthier in flesh than all the children that ate of the portion of the king's meat and drink.

> *Now at the end of the days that the king had said he should bring them in, then the prince of the eunuchs brought them in before Nebuchadnezzar. And the king communed with them; and among them all was found none like Daniel, Hananiah, Mishael, and Azariah: therefore stood they before the king.*
> *And in all matters of wisdom and understanding, that the king enquired of them, he found them ten times better than all the magicians and astrologers that were in all his realm.*
> DANIEL 1:18-20

The bottom line is that when the time came for all the teenagers to appear before the king, as the king communed with them, he found out that none of the others under his tutelage were like Daniel and his Hebrew friends. Hananiah, Mishael, and Azariah were the Babylonian names given to Shadrach, Meshach, and Abednego. They were ten times better than all other children, magicians, and astrologers in matters of wisdom and understanding. Favour brought them to that level. When you refuse the king's meat, the King of Kings will supernaturally make a way for you by His favour. They were the preferred because God's favour was on them. You don't have to compromise your faith; you don't have to cut corners. The favour of God is enough to make you stand. Depend on favour and stand for what you believe. Most people have allowed their environments and circumstances to change them. You don't have to be like them, be you and allow favour to distinguish you. Be the change in your environment, don't allow your environment to change your core values. These Hebrew boys determined to be different in a foreign land and God favoured them. Daniel reigned with four kings. He changed levels. He was influential in a foreign land by the favour of God upon him. The Hebrews had their names changed because they were captives, but their characters, values and virtues did not change. Your true name is your character, don't trade it for anything. Daniel and his three friends stood up for their beliefs, and they all excelled by divine favour. Embrace favour. It is the empowerment needed for us to make a difference. Doing right things procures favour. When you represent right things, favour will supernaturally locate you.

He that diligently seeketh good procureth favour: but he that seeketh mischief, it shall come unto him.
PROVERBS 11:27

Seeking good diligently procures favour. It is the key to procure favour and to remain in favour. Good intentions bring favour. God looks at why you are asking for favour before granting you that favour. Favour follows you naturally when you seek to be a blessing.

> *And the patriarchs, moved with envy,*
> *sold Joseph into Egypt: but God was with him,*
> *¹⁰ And delivered him out of all his afflictions, and gave him favour*
> *and wisdom in the sight of Pharaoh king of Egypt; and he made*
> *him governor over Egypt and all his house.*
> ACTS 7:9-10

Joseph was sold into slavery and taken to Egypt, but God was with him. God delivered Joseph out of all afflictions and granted him favour and wisdom in the sight of the Egyptian ruler, Pharaoh, who made him governor over Egypt and all the Pharaoh's house. It takes favour to attain such great heights. He became a prime minister in a foreign land. Favour brings influence. Favour elevates. You can't be favoured and not gain recognition. Even when Joseph was thrown into prison, he had favour with the jailer because God was with him (Genesis 39:21). You need to trust God for favour. Even in challenges, there is favour for your lifting, never be cast down because there is something about you that is different and that is favour. It will attract men and women needed for your promotion. Destiny helpers come to you by favour. Always expect favour! You are blessed and highly favoured in Jesus name.

> *Praising God, and having favour with all the people. And the Lord*
> *added to the church daily such as should be saved.*
> ACTS 2:47

As the Apostles praised, they had favour with all the people and the Lord added to the church daily such as should be saved. It takes favour to effectively witness to the lost so that they will be saved. The Lord caused the Apostles to have favour with the people, and those people were added to the church. Favour is needed for church growth. Favour draws the unsaved to receive salvation. Trust God for favour to be effective witnesses of the Gospel. People are not drawn by your looks or speech but by the favour of God radiating through you. You make impact by favour. As you deliver the mind of God in love, God supernaturally causes people to respond by favouring you in their sight.

TAKE AWAY DECLARATIONS

Father, I thank you for your unmerited favour upon my life. Today, I receive new favour in the name of Jesus.

Father, thank you for new grace and new favour, new prosperity, and blessing coming on my life.

Father, thank you for the gift of grace that guaranteed my supernatural favour. I expect to be favoured in my going out and coming in today in Jesus name.

I am well favoured as I go out today (Genesis 39-6)

I receive favour in the sight of the world (Exodus 12:36)

I shall be satisfied with your favour Oh Lord like Naphtali (Deuteronomy 33:23)

Let me have favour with you, Lord, and with men (1 Samuel 2:26)

Let me have great favour in the sight of the king (1 Samuel 16:22, 1 Kings 11:19)

Let me find favour like Esther (Esther 2:17)

Father, bless me and surround me with favour like a shield (Psalm 5:12)

Father, in the name of Jesus, I pray unto thee, that you grant me supernatural favour (Job 33:26)

My set time of favour has come. Therefore, I receive supernatural favour in everything I do in the name of Jesus (Psalm 102:13)

I am blessed and highly favoured (Luke 1:28)

PRE-CHAPTER CONVERSATION

Choice: Hello Love, how are you?

Love: I'm fine and you?

Choice: I'm good thanks. Please, can we talk?

Love: Of course. What's the matter?

Choice: Do you really love me?

Love: Of course, I love you. I have always loved you. I loved you before you realised it. From the first time I set my eyes on you, I was completely in love with you. I couldn't wait to have a date with you. I have always shown my love, and I'm still in love with you my choice. My love has been fixed on you. Why did you ask?

(This is likened to God professing His love towards you, how He loved you before you ever thought of responding to His date with you. The date was with His Son Jesus Christ who came, and you dined with Him and accepted Him. Jesus was a representative of God. God accepted you before you accepted Him).

Choice: I'm just in doubt because I feel bad sometimes thinking I have offended you and when you are upset with me, it makes me feel like you are ignoring me or neglecting me. I don't know how to explain it. When I think you are mad at me for my mistakes, my heart quakes. I think you are piling up my errors and they might explode someday. Sometimes when I say that I'm sorry, I really expect some sort of scolding or something. I'm surprised how you quickly receive me in your arms. My heart is filled with guilt and imperfection before you.

(Self-condemnation: Not knowing you have been forgiven before you even commit a sin)

Love: Oh, is that why? You don't have to think that way. I have always loved you with 100% of my love. That's with all the percentage of my love. It does not change due to what you do. I chose to love you. You are my dear choice. You were my choice even when I wasn't your choice. I chose to love you for who you are, not for what you have done or what you will do. That's who I am. That's my name, Baby. You are too precious to me for me to start looking at your flaws to determine how I should love you.

(Unconditional love depicted, she is just worried about her flaws and paying attention to them. But Love did not notice, Love loved her so much as not to look at her mistakes to determine how to treat her. Love did not allow those things to interfere with their relationship.)

Choice: Hmm, that's pretty good to know. Sorry I brought this up. It was just the way I felt.

Love: No problem. I would like to ask you the same question. Do you love me?

Choice: Yes, I do and you know I love you.

Love: Hmm, why do you think so?

Choice: You can tell Love, I have always shown my love by cooking for you, washing your clothes, tidying up the house, doing the kitchen chores, etc. I have always cared, and I try to do my best to do these works to please you.

(Choice is caught up in activities rather than relationship.)

Love: You do all these things to please me. I have been pleased with you already. I still love you whether you do these things or not. You just need to create time for us to communicate. Let's fellowship together. Let's have a long walk. Let's discuss. Let's hold hands. Let's play games.

I want more of relationship. Intimacy should come first before other things. If we don't talk, it will affect our relationship. You are starving this relationship at the expense of activities.

(Be concerned about your relationship with God more than other things. When did you pray last? Study the Word? Relate with God personally? Are you just carried away with works in God's house and tossing Him aside after service? Do you only talk to Him whenever you need to get something from Him? Are you in a walk with Him or just working for Him?)

Choice: That's true, I have not created time for adequate communication. I am always busy with work here and there! After work in the office, I come back home to continue with work.

(If you are focused only on activities, you finish your work, and you come to the house of God just to work as well, no time to talk with God. Your Bible is only opened when the pastor is teaching, after which it's closed till next church service.)

Love: That's the point. You never had time to look at my face and attend to the things of my heart. When you seek quality relationship you will be able to do your washing and house chores out of the overflow of the love in your heart, rather than working hard and not really concerned about a walk with me. It's in communication that you will know the clothes that need washing, the kind of food I would like to eat, etc.

(When you are connected in love to God's heart with understanding of His love towards you, doing the needed work will be natural to you, you won't have to be cajoled to do it. It will just flow. You will be able to do the right things, not just engage in good works.)

Choice: That's true, I will spend quality time with you. I will create the time. I want to ask another question. Why do you shower me with gifts so much? Why do we have to go on holidays, restaurants, outings, etc.?

Love: That's simple. It is because I love you and love gives. I'm just lavishing my love on you. Nothing is too much for the one I love. Do you have a problem with that?

Choice: No! Not at all. I was just thinking it's because of my efforts in trying to please you. I thought when I do all the house chores etc., that you will love me more and give me more gifts. That's why when I don't receive a gift sometimes, I start thinking I have not done enough to please you. That's why it's good to communicate. I really did not know if not that we talked about it.

(Legalism replacing relationship. Go to church because you love God not because you have to go to have attendance and to do certain things to be blessed. Be fascinated with His love for you and from that point of view serve Him in love.)

Love: My love is fixed. My blessings have been given to you. What I have is yours. My love does not fluctuate. I don't change for any reason.

(Unconditional, consistent, and fixed love)

Choice: I got it now. I will pay more attention to you rather than activities. Sometimes I work because I want you to notice me and reward me. Not knowing it's not by my works it just your nature to love, shower your blessings on me, that's why I experience the grace I have.

Thanks Love. I love you.

Love: You welcome my dearest choice. I love you more!

Chapter 6
THE LOVE DIMENSION OF GRACE

Grace originated from the love of God. God's love gave birth to grace. Without love, there would not have been grace for salvation. Understanding God's unconditional love opens you up to the grace of God. If you don't know how loved you are by God, you won't know how much grace you have been given. The law was a product of wrath while grace was a product of love. When you respond to grace by faith, you are responding to love. Without God's love, we would still be under the law. Grace brought liberation from the bondage of the law to now serving the living God in love. You can't talk about grace without talking about love. A true knowledge of God's love and getting rooted and grounded in Him loving you is one of the most important experiences you can ever have in this life. When you understand grace, you will realise that it's not based on any goodness of your own. It's just based on God's love. He loves you in spite of who you are, not because of who you are. God loved you before you were born again. He loved you before you sinned. He loved you even after you have sinned. Notice that I said 'loved'(past tense), not that He is going to love you. He has loved you. You can't do anything about it. He has been in love with you before you realised it.

> *But God commendeth his love toward us, in that,*
> *while we were yet sinners, Christ died for us.*
> ROMANS 5:8

He commended His love towards you while you were still a sinner. God loves you completely independent of yourself and your faults. You don't have to earn or deserve this love; it's totally by the grace of God. God loved you and made His grace available for you before you were born again. God's love is a fixed love. It's constant, consistent, unending and unchanging. It's not manipulatable. It's amazing how you think you can do something to make God love you. He has loved you already. The kind of love God demonstrated was because of His nature. The nature of God is the nature of love. That's who He is. God is love. Love gives, forgives, protects and chastises. In His love, we have been given salvation, we have been totally forgiven, we are protected, and we are being chastised. What you love, you protect. God is crazy about you. He thinks about you every moment of the day. He can't stop loving you. He is protective of us, and He corrects us in love. He doesn't afflict us with sickness and disease to make His corrections. He directs us by the truth of His Word. He speaks to us in love, showing us the path to take. He keeps speaking and correcting us until we get it right. He does not stop fellowshipping with us. He is never mad at us. He is patient with us and kind towards us. He does not change His mind about us.

To truly understand the attributes of God, we have to consider immeasurable love. For God is love (1 John 4:8, 16). Let us take time out to study (1 Corinthians 13:1-8) and we will see all that love is. If we substitute *God* in place of *love* in those passages, we will know what kind of love God has for us. Understanding this love will help you in your relationship with God and other people. If you don't have God's love in your heart, you cannot love your spouse or children with the love of God. It's a love that surpasses human knowledge; it's a love you have to get by revelation. The human perspective of love is limited. That's why genuine love is a scarce commodity in the world. The Holy Spirit teaches true love that is not caught; it's not a virus (Romans 5:5). We have to be taught how to love with God's kind of love. We all need to learn how to love and not to think we are at our best in loving. We are quick to love only those that love us in return, but God's kind of love loves even its enemies. You need to see by revelation God's kind of love in the light of Scriptures via the agency of the Holy Spirit. Love is not comprised of irrational, inconsistent emotions. It's not infatuation. Love is of God (1 John 4:7). It's not about your feelings; it's of God. Feelings are not reliable, but the love of God is reliable. Emotional desires can come and go, but God's love comes and stays forever. You can't trust your five senses to determine love, but God's love is trustworthy. When you see by revelation God's unconditional love, loving people regardless of their faults will be a delight. The power of the Gospel is revealed when people come to realise that regardless of what they have done, where they have been, God still loves them. God's love never gives up; it never runs out on you. It's a love that loves and keeps loving no matter what. It's consistent. God never fails because love never fails. He cannot deny himself (2 Timothy 2:13).

When you give up on God, He abides faithful. When you change, He is still there because He cannot change and deny himself. God lives and stays in love. He is true to who He is. He is the same yesterday, today and forevermore. Behold what manner of love the Father has lavished on us that we should be called the sons of God (1 John 3:1). God lavished great love on us that brought us to sonship. We were all lost, but now found in His love and grace. Dear Valued Ones, God loves you. If you could grasp His love by revelation, it would solve all of life's issues. You would see that God is not against you, that He is for you and if God is for you who can be against you?

> *In this was manifested the love of God toward us,*
> *because that God sent his only begotten Son into the world,*
> *that we might live through him.*
>
> [10] *Herein is love, not that we loved God, but that he loved us,*
> *and sent his Son to be the propitiation for our sins.*
> I JOHN 4:9-10

None of us was worth God sending His Son to die in our place. No one deserves the love of God. Still, He manifested His love towards us.

He sent a treasured possession to redeem the world back to Himself. He paid a very costly price to prove His love for us. Notice that it was stated in the above Scripture, "not that we loved God, but that He loved us and sent His Son to be the propitiation for our sins." Jesus was the peace offering that atoned for our sins and reconciled us back to God. That is how genuine love should act. Genuine love loves its haters. If you don't know God's kind of love, you will not truly know how to love. God loved you while you were His enemy. The natural man loves only when it's reciprocated, but God loved you when you did not reciprocate His love. Instead, you were against Him.

IDENTIFYING WITH YOUR TRUE IDENTITY

> *For all have sinned, and come short of the glory of God;*
> *Being justified freely by his grace through*
> *the redemption that is in Christ Jesus:*
> ROMANS 3:23-24

In Adam, we have all sinned and were doomed for condemnation. We all deserved God's wrath in Adam. We had an identification with Adam that brought us death, sin, sickness, poverty, failure, condemnation and guilt. We were conceived in sin. We were born into sin by Adam; we can only be born out of sin by Christ. He was released for you and I. What Adam did affected the whole of humanity. What Adam and Jesus Christ did affected the whole universe. One affected us negatively, and the other affected us positively. We had fallen out of God's glory. We all missed it in the loins of Adam. Jesus came to affect us positively. He is the last Adam. He came on a rescue mission to a dying world. We now have a new identity with Christ that has brought us life, righteousness, blessings, justification and prosperity. We are justified, just as if we never sinned, as if we have done nothing. In God's eyes, we appear as one that has never having sinned because of what Jesus did for us. Our Adamic nature of sin was lost on the cross. A new nature of righteousness was given to us by Jesus Christ. God justified us freely by His grace.

You are no longer who you used to be. God does not see you the way you see yourself. You have to start seeing yourself the way God sees you. What you did before your salvation is irrelevant. There was an old you, and now there is a new you. A brand-new you (II Corinthians 5:17). You are living now as if you have never existed before, as a new species. This happened freely without your input; you did not do anything to receive salvation except by exercising your faith. Jesus paid the price (redemption), and you simply received the prize (salvation).

> *But God, who is rich in mercy, for his great love*
> *wherewith he loved us,*
> *⁵ Even when we were dead in sins, hath quickened us together*
> *with Christ, (by grace ye are saved;)*
> EPHESIANS 2:4-5

Grace is an expression of God's great love towards us. If not for the richness of God's mercy and love there would not have been grace. For God so loved the world that He gave His only begotten son (John 3:16). Love is the root of grace. Love gave us grace. God's great love for us gave birth to the great grace that brought us salvation. Embrace His love for you.

> *For he hath made him to be sin for us, who knew no sin;*
> *that we might be made the righteousness of God in him.*
> 2 CORINTHIANS 5:21

God made Jesus, who knew no sin, to be sin so that you might become the righteousness of God now in Christ. You have been justified and made righteous by grace. This happened by the love God bestowed on us. Everything has been done and settled in your spirit man. You need to start responding to the real you and your new reality of God's righteousness, justification and blessings. There is a new you and you have to start living as becomes you. Live out the real you. The devil tries to rob you of your true identity in Christ, not who you looked like in Adam. It is in identifying with your true self in Christ that you start acting like Him. Who you are is determined by what Christ has done.

Your relevance is in Him. What you have done or what you will do does not change your new nature of righteousness in Christ. You have been made already; you can't be unmade. Can you unmake what God has made? You can't. You have been made righteous by God in Christ. Just respond to who you are by faith. Express on the outside what has been done on your inside. Give expression to the real you by faith. When you make a mistake don't stay in it, stand up and repent of your sin. Continue in a loving relationship with God.

STAY IN A LOVING RELATIONSHIP AND NOT IN RELIGION

It is very easy to be caught up in works rather than to maintain a walk with Christ. There are lots of things we engage in that are very right but are done with the wrong motives and knowledge. Nothing is as stinky as wrong knowledge. It's destructive. Having the right knowledge and right application of that knowledge makes you wise. Seek not just to acquire knowledge, but to acquire the right knowledge.

God wants a relationship, not religion. It's easy to shift focus from God by trying to do things to get God to love us and to find favour in His sight and thinking we are going to be blessed by our works. Relationship is the heartbeat of God, not religion. He has loved you with an everlasting love (Jeremiah 31:3). He will not change for any reason. He wants you to respond to His love and He wants you to fellowship with Him. Let all you do be moderated by your respond to love. Love motivates you. You are so fascinated by His love for you, and now you love Him in return. You were blessed two thousand years ago, don't be carried away by service to God to be blessed. He has blessed you. Do what you do by love and in response to the finished work of Christ for you. Stay in love and stay out of religion.

Legalism has gradually crept into the Church of Christ. When you do things to win God's favour, to deserve God's blessing, you are operating in legalism. Christ has dealt with the law. God will not love you more because you work more. He has loved you already. He wants you to do all you do in love. God has loved you and has proven His love with an A+ result by sending His son to die for you and me. Your salvation, deliverance, prosperity, healing, blessings, divine favour and all-around success were released by the process. Christ died for all your provisions in Him. Reciprocate His love and stay in a loving relationship with Him. He has given you all things to enjoy. Don't try to work for what has already been worked out. It affects your relationship with God. Do what you do because you love Him, not because you want Him to love and bless you. He has done all there is to be done. The cross was a finished work. Nothing was left undone. Get your motives right in your walk with God so that you can truly enjoy God and His blessings. God has let go of His heart and hand completely to you by the finished work of Christ. Unfortunately, we only seek Him for His hand and not His heart. Don't serve God because of what He has to offer you. What would God withhold from you if He did not withhold His Son from coming to earth to die for you? All other things are fringe benefits of what Jesus did. It's a done deal. Don't misinterpret it. Go for relationship and all other things will be additions (Matthew 6:33). Go for the interest of the King of Kings. Seek first the Kingdom with all you heart and watch things just fall in place for you effortlessly. Do things from the standpoint of a heart for God, not a heart for the hand of God.

> *For this is the love of God, that we keep his commandments:*
> *and his commandments are not grievous.*
> I JOHN 5:3

If you truly understand God's unconditional love towards you, your obedience to God now will be born out of your love for God. Therefore, His commandments will no longer be grievous. You will just delight in obeying God now. The commandments of God are grievous if you are doing something to get God to love you, if you are doing out of law instead of love for God or if you are doing something to be accepted and blessed by God. It becomes grievous, but if you know you have been loved and accepted already in the Beloved, obeying God becomes a delightsome adventure. Relationship should come before things. Doing things out of regulations will be tiring and weary, but doing things out of love will be exciting. Just love God. Stay in a loving relationship with Him and celebrate Him for His goodness and blessings that have been released. Love Him in all you do. Respond to and with true love, and do not serve God on conditions. If He should strictly require conditions from you to love, bless and accept you, you can't meet the benchmark. Therefore you can never qualify for His love, blessings and be accepted by your works. His standard was too high to be met. It was a perfect, flawless standard that we could not meet and Jesus was sent to meet all God's standards. We are only enjoying what we would have worked for. We are resting in the finished work of Christ on the cross.

> *And if by grace, then is it no more of works: otherwise grace is no more grace. But if it be of works, then it is no more grace: otherwise work is no more work.*
> ROMANS 11:6

If it's by grace, it means it is no more of works. Grace and works do not mix. If it's grace, it should be grace through faith completely, and if it's law, it should be by works completely. The law was by works to win God's acceptance, blessings and approval. God gave the Old Testament law to expose how ungodly we were, to bring us to the end of ourselves. The law condemns. It was tough to abide because no one could keep all the law. The law was not just the Ten Commandments; it was all that was given to Moses by God. It comprised the first five books of the Bible (Pentateuch). It was given to humble man and to bring man to the end of himself. Only when you come to the end of yourself will you truly find the beginning of God and know that you can't help yourself any longer than to seek a saviour. You can now say, "Oh Lord; it's no longer of me, it has got to be you." The law was a guide or path to the savour (Jesus Christ). Then grace came along, and you were accepted, loved, blessed and forgiven. Go now and express who you are and fellowship with God in love, not in fear of what you are going to do to get Him to move in your direction. God moved on your behalf two thousand years ago.

Faith is your positive respond to the divine provision (grace) that God has made available in Christ. Lots of questions may be running through your mind now. The answers are in the Word. Just read carefully. Have you ever asked why Christ said, "It is finished" at the cross? Why He came and went to the cross? Why He died that way instead of by some other means? What was finished on the cross was the law, your sickness, diseases, barrenness, sin, condemnation, punishment and poverty. He was made a curse for us so that the covenant of blessing can rest upon us (Galatians 3:13-14).

> *As ye have therefore received Christ Jesus the Lord, so walk ye in him: ⁷ Rooted and built up in him, and stablished in the faith, as ye have been taught, abounding therein with thanksgiving.*
> COLOSSIANS 2:6-7

Two thousand years ago, long before you were born, Jesus bore the sins of the world. When you heard the good news of the grace of God, you just reached out to it by faith and appropriated it. I started with that to cast your mind back to how it all started. You did nothing to get the work of grace to start in your direction, you only responded by faith to this great love that was lavished on you. Now you have received grace; all things have been done for you on a platter of grace. You did not work for it; you did not earn it; you did not pay for it; you only received it.

But now you have become religious; you have started trying to earn things. As you have therefore received Christ Jesus the Lord, so walk ye in Him. In the same way you received Him, continue in that manner. Don't do otherwise. Walk in Him the same way you received Him. How did you walk? In other words, how did you come into salvation? What were you doing right to qualify for salvation? If you did not qualify for it, don't work to qualify for it. Maintain your work in the simple faith of the finished work of Christ. It is already a done deal. Don't make complex what God has made simple, thereby putting yourself in struggles and legalism. Have a love mentality as opposed to work mentality. You may be doing good things like fasting, praying and studying the Word of God, but if your motives are to merit God's favour and blessings, you will be disappointed. These things are good, but they should be done with the right motives. If you are motivated by love, you will see the difference. Be intrigued with love and how blessed you have become in Christ. Abound in the fullness of what has been done by thanking God for it. When you focus on your performance, then your faith is no longer in the unconditional love of God that made all things available to you by grace. If you focus on how holy you have been living, your faith is no longer of grace. Stop for a moment and be realistic. Have you ever thought that you needed to do certain things to get certain blessings? If so, you are relying on yourself to get through to God. You are still depending on what you can offer to be blessed. Can you buy what Christ has bought for you? He has done it all.

Most people live in a world of do's and don'ts with God, and grace has been tossed aside. It is a great thing to pray, fast, read the Word of God, attend church and tithe, but don't do them to affect God. God's love for you is not based on what you do. He saved you because you were worth saving. He didn't save you due to some goodness in your life. Your holiness or lack of it does not change God's heart towards you. God loved you before you were holy. God does not withdraw His love because you are not acting holy enough. Your holiness will change your heart towards God. Studying the Word will change your heart towards God. You will know Him better and relate with Him appropriately. Renew your mind with the Word of God and be aware of the provisions that God has made available for you. Mix your faith with it. You cannot make God answer your prayers by doing enough right things. If you are fasting, fast because you are going to put your flesh under subjection and be more sensitive to God for fellowship, or to war against the devil and fleshly desires. Fasting changes us, but does not change God's mind on issues. Fasting is not a pathway of merit for God's blessings. It should be done under the new covenant grace, not under the old covenant law and not to get God to move or speak. Fasting increases our spiritual capacity, breaks habits and spiritual bondages. It helps you to discern what the Holy Spirit is already saying to your spirit and brings more intimacy with Him. Fasting brings you to focus and clarity to what the Lord is already saying.

When you pray, don't allow your prayer to be geared at changing God towards you, let it be geared towards you changing into who God has destined you to be in Christ and receiving what God has already done by faith.

When you tithe, do so because you want to honour God and worship Him with your offering, not just because you want to make a transaction. Love Him with your offerings. It is also a proof of your faith in the covenant of blessing that He has made on your behalf. If you don't give, it doesn't mean that God is upset with you and will make you spend your money on hospital bills. No! It means that you are not interested in financial prosperity and you have pegged down your finances by yourself. God is not to blame. He is not angry with you. Your tithing will allow to rebuke devourers for your sake and cause you to experience financial explosion.

When rendering service in the house of God, do it because you love Him and because He has blessed you with the ability to do it. If you refuse to go to church, it does not change God's love for you, but it affects you. It's lack of wisdom to stay away from what makes you grow in your relationship with God. It's for your own good and does not affect God in any way. Church is your place of strengthening and service where you get cleansed and renewed by the Word. Just respond to love and grace by faith.

> *But after that the kindness and love of God our Saviour toward man appeared, Not by works of righteousness which we have done, but according to his mercy he saved us, by the washing of regeneration, and renewing of the Holy Ghost;*
> TITUS 3:4-5

God demonstrated His kindness and love towards man. It was not by works of righteousness which we have done, but according to His mercy that He saved us. We were saved by grace through faith. It is not by our righteous deeds, it was by His mercy that we are saved. Continue to live this new life by faith in the finished works of Christ.

> *O foolish Galatians, who hath bewitched you,*
> *that ye should not obey the truth, before whose eyes Jesus Christ hath*
> *been evidently set forth, crucified among you?*
> *This only would I learn of you, Received ye the Spirit by the works*
> *of the law, or by the hearing of faith? Are ye so foolish? having*
> *begun in the Spirit, are ye now made perfect by the flesh?*
> GALATIANS 3:1-3

Paul speaking to the Galatians might have sounded like this in modern vernacular: "Oh foolish Galatians! What magician has hypnotised you and cast an evil spell on you that you can no longer see clearly the purpose of the death of Christ? How did you receive the Spirit? Was it by the works of the law, or by the hearing of faith? Are you so foolish? Not realising how you started? If you started in the Spirit, are you now going to be made perfect by the flesh? You should continue just the way you started. You started by faith in the finished work of Christ in your spirit, so continue by faith. You are made perfect in your spirit man by the finished work of Christ through the agency of the Holy Spirit. Don't struggle for perfection any longer, respond to your perfected spirit. You are perfect in your spirit. You can't be made perfect by the works of your flesh. You will get tired."

> *For in Jesus Christ neither circumcision availeth any thing, nor*
> *uncircumcision; but faith which worketh by love.*
> GALATIANS 5:6

When you come to an understanding of God's unconditional love, your faith is boosted up. Faith works by love. Your faith should be fuelled by God's love for you. Being overwhelmed by that love is what energises your faith to function effectively. If you know the length, breadth, width and height of God's love, you can trust Him for anything. Christ loved you enough to bear your sins, suffer the shame and die for you on the cross. It all started with love. You cannot talk about trust without love. It's only when you are in love that you can talk about trust. If you want to trigger your faith for exploits, get intoxicated with God's love. Your faith only comes alive when your understanding of His unconditional love for you comes alive. Walk in a loving relationship with God after knowing how much He has loved you. He is still in love with you until the end of the world. He will never leave you nor forsake you (Hebrews 13:5). Whatsoever is not of faith is sin (Romans 14:23) and sin is the transgression of the law. If you want to work for things to be loved and to be qualified for God's blessing, you will find yourself in sin because you will no longer be walking by faith. Faith is resting in the finished work of Christ. Acknowledge God's love and stay in a loving relationship with Him.

YOU ARE TOTALLY FORGIVEN

Sometimes miracles are limited because although people believe God exists and He is able to do it, they don't believe in His willingness to move in their direction due to feelings of guilt and condemnation of sin. Most people think that God offers you forgiveness of all your sins committed up till the time you get born-again. He did it before you realised it. When you accepted Jesus Christ, your past sins were forgiven. However every sin you commit after that time has to be dealt with, you repent of every sin and take cover under the blood of Jesus.

God has forgiven all your sins, past, present and future. Even the sins you haven't committed yet have already been forgiven (Hebrews 10:10, 12 & 14, 1 John 2:2). Your salvation, God's love for you, His willingness to heal you, and to use you and answer your prayer are not tied to you getting every sin confessed. If that was the case, it would have been better for you to die immediately when you gave your life to Christ so that you would make heaven. While you are here on earth, you will be faced with sin, either by omission or commission. It could be by actions, by words or by thoughts. Sin is sin. There is no mega-sin nor micro-sin. Thank God for His total forgiveness of our sin in Christ. It's now your responsibility to confess any known sin and acknowledge your sin to God by saying, "Lord, you were right. I was wrong." Name your sins and turn from them. By confessing you kick the devil away. You are drawing into your body and soul the righteousness and holiness that exist already in your born-again spirit. This will drive the devil nuts, and he will take off from your life. Even though you gave the devil a legal right to come into your life by yielding to sin in the first place, by confessing and turning away from it, you give expression to the power (grace) that is located in your spirit to come out and cleanse you from all unrighteousness (I John 1:9). That's it, amongst all other definitions of grace as we have come to understand is that: Grace is divine resistance to sin through the power of the Holy Ghost in your spirit when you yield to it. It is also an empowerment to make you stand in the face of challenges. You have been totally forgiven in Christ. You are now a candidate for heaven. You confess your sins to prevent the devil from derailing you and to get it right with God. Sin is destructive, it retards you, it hardens your heart. Sin is a sinker; it sinks destinies. It makes you go cold, insensitive, unyielding and unfeeling towards God. (Hebrews 3:13). It stings you with pains and regrets. It's an emotional response in wrong directions. When you sin, you can't see or perceive properly. You become dull in your spirit and lose perception. Sin has consequences. However, these consequences are not of God but of the devil. The devil takes advantage of sin to afflict you. But God is a Spirit, and He is looking at you in the spirit (John 4:24, Hebrews 12:9). God corrects you in love, He doesn't condemn you or punish you for anything, even when you have sinned and given the devil access into your life. God's love for you never fluctuates. He loves you just as much as He ever did. He does not love you because you are lovely. He loves you because He is love. That's who He is towards you. In His love, you have been completely forgiven. This is not to encourage sin but to point out the truth. I'm not a fan of sin. I hate sin. I don't live in sin. Since I learned what grace was, I maximised it in my life. I have not arrived yet, but I have taken off. I'm not where I used to be. My walk with God has been glorious. I want you to get this understanding, it will help you move away from your mistakes and not wallow in sin. When you make mistakes, face up to them and run to God, not from God. The devil has caught people in his web, and many are stuck there having wrong perception about God's love for them. A true understanding of God's grace does not encourage sin. It breaks the backbone of sin.

> *Or despisest thou the riches of his goodness*
> *and forbearance and longsuffering; not knowing that the goodness of*
> *God leadeth thee to repentance?*
> ROMANS 2:4

Knowing the goodness of God is what leads to repentance, not the teaching of condemnation. You don't draw people to God by condemning them. God does not condemn. When you know that you have been eternally loved and forgiven, you will come to the place of repentance. You will want to walk in a loving relationship with the Lord. By His love for you, you were totally forgiven.

> *To the praise of the glory of his grace, wherein he hath made us*
> *accepted in the beloved.*
> EPHESIANS 1:6

The glory of His grace has made you to be accepted in the Beloved. By the love of God that was manifested through His grace, we were all accepted two thousand years ago. We need not crave God's acceptance. We have been accepted. God chose to accept us back to Himself by grace. He did that by sending Christ to die for us. He received us back in Christ Jesus. Imagine how your relationship with God will be more glorious when you accept this truth.

> *He that spared not his own Son, but delivered him up for us all,*
> *how shall he not with him also freely give us all things?*
> ROMANS 8:32

This Scripture says it all! Why kill yourself over things that have been freely given to you? With the giving of Christ to you, everything else was released to you as well. It's a lack of understanding that makes it seem as if you are getting God to do things for you. He has handled everything on the cross. You have been totally forgiven on the cross; you have been healed on the cross, you have been blessed on the cross, you have been made righteous on the cross, you have been delivered on the cross. It all happened freely with no works on your part to get anything done. If you know that you are forgiven and loved by God, then being healed is insignificant. It has been dealt with. If you are struggling to believe that God will heal you, bless you, deliver you, give you that breakthrough, you are really struggling with the love of God. Knowing God's love is what gives your faith the strength to believe God for anything. Since He did not keep Jesus from going to the cross for you, what do you think He is keeping from you now? It is God's will for everybody to be healed (III John 1:2).

> *Every good gift and every perfect gift is from above,*
> *and cometh down from the Father of lights, with whom is no*
> *variableness, neither shadow of turning.*
> JAMES 1:17

Every good and perfect gift is from above. It's God's will for you to be healed. It is God's will for you to receive your breakthrough. God is not against you. It is best to turn around sometimes after praying, and if the answer is not forthcoming, to ask what is really wrong. Ask God to show you what is standing against your breakthrough. From meditation, you will find out the devil is behind it. Then you can rebuke the devil and get your deliverance and breakthroughs. God is not the problem or obstacle. God is constant; He is not variable in His dealings. There is no shadow of turning with Him, no change of mind. He wants it done. You might need to speak to the mountain to see it done. Your miracles have happened on the cross. It's good news that we are living in the reality of what He has done by faith. Our faith is to live in the reality of what He has been done. Your faith reaches out and appropriates the finished work of Christ.

> *For the grace of God that bringeth salvation*
> *hath appeared to all men,*
> [12] *Teaching us that, denying ungodliness and worldly lusts, we*
> *should live soberly, righteously, and godly, in this present world;*
> TITUS 2:11-12

The grace of God teaches you to live a sober, righteous and holy life. The grace of God does not permit you to keep sinning. It breaks the backbone of sin from your life. When you understand God's unconditional love for you, you will naturally want to live a godly life. That's the way you can truly understand grace and maximise it by a faith response. If you grasp a revelation of God's unconditional love, you will serve God more accidentally than you ever did on purpose. It will flow with freshness. Your performance will be motivated by love instead of by works.

TAKE AWAY DECLARATIONS

Thank you, Lord, for your great love towards me. It's so amazing. I'm saturated with your love.

I am the apple of your eye. Your love for me never gives up on me, it never fails and never runs out on me. It's like a hurricane.

I am loved with an everlasting love (Jeremiah 31:3)

I have been accepted in Christ the beloved (Ephesians 1:6)

I will do anything you want me to do because I love you so much. Your commandments are not grievous to me. It's my delight to serve your interest, no matter what it will cost because you first loved me. (I John 5:3 & 4:19)

I have been made perfect and totally forgiven of my sins (Hebrews 10:14)

My faith is working because of my understanding of your love for me. I believe in your love for me, and I can trust you for anything. (Galatians 5:6)

I don't try to serve in your vineyard for you to love me, I serve you because I'm responding to your love for me. I'm indebted to your love for me. I can't love you enough. I'm just in love with you, and I will love you forever.

I will love others because I know what true love is from your kind of love towards me.

I want to develop an intimate relationship with you.

PRE-CHAPTER STORY

This story comes from Luke 15 in the New Testament, the story of the prodigal son.

A man had two sons. The younger told his father…

Jamie: Father, I want my share of your estate now. I want my portion of my inheritance.

(He couldn't wait till the father died, though that was rude. He requested his inheritance immediately. His father agreed and divided his wealth between his sons. He gave a part to Jamie who asked, and the other part to Jude that did not ask. A few days later Jamie, the younger son, packed all his belongings and took a trip to a distant land, and there he wasted all his money on parties and prostitutes. About the time his money was gone, a great famine swept over the land, and he began to starve. He persuaded a local farmer to hire him to feed his pigs. The farmer agreed. He started his new job. He became so hungry that even the pig's food looked good for him to eat. No one gave him food to eat. Jamie finally came back to his senses after meditation. He said to himself much like the prodigal son said in the Bible, "At home even the hired men have food enough and to spare, and I am dying of hunger. I will go to my father and say, 'Father, I have sinned against both heaven and you and am no longer worthy to be called your son, please take me on as a hired man.'" He returned home, and while he was still a long distance away, his father saw him coming, and was filled with loving pity and ran and embraced him and kissed him. That's what unconditional love can do.)

Father, I have sinned against heaven and you and am not worthy of being called your son.

(While he was still talking, his father was calling on the servants)

Father: Bring the finest robe in the house and put it on him and a jewelled ring for his finger; and shoes. Kill the calf we have in the fattening pen. We must celebrate with a feast. For my son was dead and has returned to life. He was lost and is found.

(The party started. Meanwhile, Jude the older son, who had been in the fields working, returned home. He heard dance music coming from the house, and he asked one of the servants):

Jude: What's going on here?

Servant: Your brother is back, and your father has killed the calf we were fattening and has prepared a great feast to celebrate his safe arrival.

(Jude was so angry and wouldn't go into the house, he stood outside angrily.)

(Father noticed and came out to beg him to no avail.)

Jude: All these years I've served you, I have worked hard for you and never transgressed at any time your commandments, and in all that time you never gave me even one young goat for a feast with my friends. Yet when this son of yours comes back after spending your money on prostitutes, you celebrate by killing the finest calf we have on the place.

Father: Look, dear son, you have been with me, and all that I have is yours. It is right to celebrate. For he is your brother, and he was dead and has come back to life! He was lost and is found.

Note: Jamie was a rebellious son who was accepted back by the father with unconditional love. The father loved him irrespective of what he did. The father celebrated his return; he was not angry with him. He did not scold him as one would expect. He did not have to punish him before accepting him back. The father saw him from a far distance, meaning he was watching for the son and had been looking forward to seeing him.

The father ran out in love with open arms to receive him. Jamie was trying to explain; the father did not give time for explanations. He threw a party for him immediately. The father had forgiven the son long before the son came to his senses. He had been loved, and the love had not been susceptible to change.

Jude was a religious son who was concerned about service and conscious of his right doings. He explained to his father that he had served all these years and had never transgressed his father's commandments, but the father have never given him this kind of feast. Relationship was lacking. He was work-conscious and was looking to his works to win the father's blessings. The father replied that Jude had been with him and all the father had was Jude's property now. The father had already blessed the son. There was no work that the son could do to be blessed any more, the blessing was already done. Let's have relationship with God. How can you be in a house full of your inheritance and never make a request for anything that belongs to you? Why did the son not realise he had already been blessed with everything? He was just supposed to reach out by faith to get what belonged to him. He was religious, that's why! He missed out on what he could have enjoyed. If he had requested to kill any calf at any time, nobody would have stopped him. All things are ready for the taking by grace. You did not work for them, don't work to enjoy them.

Chapter 7

WE ARE ALREADY BLESSED BY GRACE

We are already blessed by grace. God anticipated all we would ever need and made it available by the finished work of Christ two thousand years ago. He poured His blessings on us. He has been into your future and envisaged your needs. Therefore, He made a supply for those needs by the death and resurrection of Jesus Christ. You are only evolving into all He has done in your spirit through Christ Jesus. All you need is to believe and receive. As a born-again child of God, you are not trying to get blessed. You are already blessed in your spirit. If Jesus had not come to earth and died and resurrected for you, you would be permitted to live in sickness, disease, poverty, curses, failure, barrenness, and retrogression. What He did, He did for you, not for Himself. Glory to God that He was released for you and me and He has brought us blessings, divine health, prosperity, success, fruitfulness, and progress. All that needed to be done to make you a blessed man has been done already. Reach out with faith to take delivery of your own package. If you understand the impact of the blessings bestowed upon you, you will never struggle. God is not keeping anything from you; He is not hiding anything from you, He has given you everything. It's time to draw out those blessings from spiritual to physical manifestation. You are so loaded in your spirit. This is not to excite you but to insight you. It is an insight into your new reality in Christ. It is not wise to try to use your faith to get God to do what He has already done. If you have a son and you have given him your estate and all that belongs to you, he has the keys. All you have has been declared his. Would it not be absurd for him to meet you and start begging for you to give him the estate? To ask you to give him the car you have given him already? Why ask for what has been categorically given to you? As his father, you might ask this son what part of "I have already given everything to you" he doesn't understand. God is asking what part of "it is finished" don't you understand? (John 19:30). Jesus Christ did a finished work on the cross. If he has done it, then it is done. That settles it. It is your responsibility to know what you want and just reach out to get it by faith. If there is any opposition on your way, you address it by the authority that has been given to you in Christ. The only thing that could be standing in your way of breakthrough is the devil, he is here to oppose you. He does not want you to enjoy what God has done for you. You have been given the authority and power to kick the devil out of your affairs so that you can enjoy your blessings. Most times instead of speaking to and addressing our mountains, we start begging God in prayers to do what He has already done. You are already endowed in your spirit with all it will take to live a successful life. Make discoveries from the Word of God to know whatever has been made available for you in Christ and take delivery of them. It is easier if you know them already. Just start appropriating them by faith, and speak to whatever is contrary to what has being done for you. Your faith is not to get God to move in your direction; God has moved already in your direction through Christ. Your faith is to move mountains that are standing in your way of getting what God has done for you. Reach out by faith to get what is yours. Your faith doesn't move God; God has already moved on your behalf in grace. Your faith will move mountains in your life and move you into position to receive the great grace that has been made available for you in Christ. We are saved and blessed by what Jesus did on the cross, and our response to that reality is our faith. Faith simply appropriates what is already done in the death, burial, and resurrection of Jesus Christ (grace). Faith receives and responds to grace. Faith is a receiver of what grace has transmitted. You are responding to the goodness of God by faith. You are walking by faith receiving all the blessings that have been bought and paid for by Jesus Christ. Anything you will ever need is already available in Christ. God is not creating anything new now, you are only receiving what He has created for you by His grace through faith.

> *Blessed be the God and Father of our Lord Jesus Christ, who hath blessed us with all spiritual blessings in heavenly places in Christ:*
> EPHESIANS 1:3

We can see from Scriptures that God's blessing upon us is not what He's going to do. It is what He has done already. All means all, no remainder. It's a done deal. You might be asking why spiritual blessings, why not physical blessings? It is spiritual blessings because what Christ did was done in your spirit. It's faith that transmits it to the physical realm. Faith is your spiritual converter that converts spiritual blessings to physical reality. Just because you have not seen it in the physical doesn't mean it has not taken place. It has taken place already; you are only going to reach out to it by faith to enjoy it. A misuse of your faith can make you miss out on the best of God's provisions in Christ. Go for the blessing with faith. It's now up to you, no longer up to God. The faith that makes God totally responsible for your blessing is a false faith. Real faith believes God for what He has done and reaches out to receive what has been given. Faith is a responsibility on your part to go all out for what God has done through the finished work of Christ. It's not faith if it's waiting on God to start all over again to start doing things He has already done. Christ cannot die again. Your faith should believe that God has done it and you go for it. Your blessings are established in Christ already. Most people believe that God can do anything, but they don't believe He has already done it. Instead of believing in what the Bible says has already been done, many people spend their lives pursuing God, trying to beg Him to do something. Put off the tradition of "one day things will be fine," God will do it, it's God's will, He will do it when He wants to do it, it's up to God, etc. The truth is that He has done it. Don't debate it, decide today to use your faith to get what Christ has done for you. If you need to resist the devil, resist the devil and contend for what has been given. The devil is your enemy; he does not want you to enjoy what God has given you. Receive your healing, receive your deliverance, receive your miracles, receive your breakthrough and promotions. They are all yours. If it's up to God only, then He would have done it because it's His will that you are blessed. It's not God's will to see you suffer. Now that He has perfected His will in Christ Jesus through His finished work, don't you think you are left with some duties of believing in what has been done? Another question you might be asking is whether what God has done exists only in heavenly places. You should know that in the spirit realm you have changed kingdoms. You have been translated from the kingdom of darkness into the Kingdom of God's Dear Son (Colossians 1:13). Though you live in this world, you are no longer of this world. You belong to a new kingdom which is the kingdom of light.

> *Blessed be the God and Father of our Lord Jesus Christ, who hath blessed us with all spiritual blessings in heavenly places in Christ:*
> EPHESIANS 2:6

We have been raised up together with Christ. When He died, we died, when He resurrected, we resurrected with Him. He has brought us to heavenly places. We don't need to get to heaven to experience heaven. We have already started living it out here. It's a heaven on earth experience. We are only going to continue when we get to heaven. We have a dual citizenship that has the capacity of living in two worlds at the same time: the spiritual world and the physical world. We are in this present world right now, but we are not of this world. You are born again; you have the life of Christ in you. Jesus has brought heaven to the earth because He resides in you, so you are now a resident of heaven while you are still here. Our spirit man is operating in heavenly places in earthly realms. This is what confers in us the dominion needed to dominate on earth. You are expected to draw your blessings from the spiritual realm to earthly realm. Don't settle for less when you have heaven's best at your disposal.

> *The eyes of your understanding being enlightened;*
> *that ye may know what is the hope of his calling,*
> *and what the riches of the glory of his inheritance **in the saints**,*
> *And what is the exceeding greatness of his power to us-ward who*
> *believe, according to the working of his mighty power,*
> *Which he wrought in Christ, when he raised him from the dead,*

and set him at his own right hand in the heavenly places,
Far above all principality, and power, and might, and dominion,
and every name that is named, not only in this world,
but also in that which is to come:
EPHESIANS 1:18-21

In Paul's prayer to the Ephesians, he was so concerned that he had to pray for them in this manner. He did not pray for God to bless them, to prosper them, to give them breakthroughs. Not at all, Paul prayed that the eyes of their understanding be enlightened that they may know why they were called and the riches of the glory of His inheritance in the Saints, the riches that have been deposited inside the Saints. In other words, you are rich in your spirit! Paul was praying that they would have the revelation of what has already be done, that their understanding should be opened to know how blessed they were in the spirit and to know what is the exceeding greatness of His power (grace) towards them who believe. There is superabundant power on your inside as a born-again child of God. It's the power of grace. It is God's ability to change you and circumstances around you. This power is what you need to change your world. It is the power Jesus has brought to us to have a heaven on earth experience. This is the same power that was wrought in Christ when God raised Him from the dead and set Him at His own right hand in the heavenly places where we belong by identification. It's strictly for believers, not unbelievers. There is excess power in your spirit. The power that raised up Jesus from the dead dwells in you. The power you need is not farfetched; it's already in you. The blessing you need is already in you. The riches of the glory of His inheritance are not going to come tomorrow; you have them in you already. The power is meant to resist the devil, and he will flee. If you don't know how powerful you are, the devil will take advantage of you. You have the resistant, to resist him and contend with him in the battle against your inheritance (Deuteronomy 2:24). Contend with the devil in battle. Command things to change. The devil has had a fight with God, and God won hands down. God gave you the victory and empowerment needed to face anything. The devil is now all out against you. He is against all that God has done in Christ.

You can see from the above Scripture that you have been placed far above the devil. Your new status changed your sitting level, from a low chair to a high chair. You have been elevated. You have to engage in battle against any attempt to stop your blessing, breakthrough, miracle, fruitfulness, success, and prosperity by using this understanding. You have been given excessive power in your spirit. Respond to it! Use your authority to speak to your challenges. Face your mountains and enjoy a fountain of blessings. Don't allow the devil to have fun in stopping you when you can give him problems he cannot recover from. He has lost, he has no power over your spirit, he fights against your body and mind. When you are afflicted in those areas, react aggressively in the spirit to see what you have been given manifest in the physical. You have been blessed and empowered in your spirit already. God has done everything he wants to do through Jesus.

According as his divine power hath given unto us all things that pertain unto life and godliness, through the knowledge of him that hath called us to glory and virtue:
II PETER 1:3

God has given unto us all things that pertain to life and godliness. The divine power of God's grace has made all things available to us in Christ. We are not struggling for these things; we have them already. They have all been done in the past. Our knowledge of Jesus Christ and what He has done awakens us to draw from this fountain of blessings on the inside. We are to be conscious that what we are chasing after God to do for us has been done. We just need to start stretching out by faith to receive what He has done. We are called to a life of glory and virtue. You can't see this glory and virtue if you don't believe it has been released. He has given unto us all things (past tense), Him that hath called us to glory and virtue (past tense). Your faith is meant for you to live in the reality of what has been done already. Grace has provided us with all things. It's already Yours!

And he said unto him, Son, thou art ever with me, and all that I have is thine.
LUKE 15:31

The father in speaking to the older son in the parable of the prodigal son said, "Son thou art with me, and all that I have is yours." The boy lacked understanding; he did not know that all the father had ever worked for had been declared his. He was blessed already, but he did not know. It is possible to be blessed and not know it. If you don't know, you will struggle unnecessarily. You will think you have to labour for the blessing. He was ever with the Father, in a wealthy place but had never touched anything for his own use. He was working hard for the father; always in the field thinking the father would bless him some day if he was pleased with the son's output. He didn't know that the father was waiting for him to make some moves. The father was waiting for him to come up with the idea of killing a fattened calf for celebrating. The son was waiting for the father. God will not withhold any good thing from you. He has given you all things. Place a demand on what has been given by grace. You can be so caught up in activity like this religious boy that you miss out on God's best if you don't know what He has done for you. It's yours already. What you are asking God for is yours already. God has given to you all things to enjoy. God has made all His blessings yours by salvation.

Salvation belongeth unto the Lord:
thy blessing is upon thy people. Selah.
PSALM 3:8

Salvation is of the Lord. It is the Lord that gives salvation and with salvation comes God's blessing upon you. The grace of God that brings salvation has appeared to all man (Titus 2:11). Grace brought salvation and with salvation comes God's blessing. God did not only save you, but He also blessed you. You have received salvation by simple faith in the finished work of Christ. Your blessing is determined also by your faith in the finished work of Christ. He has blessed you. God's blessing is upon His people. Every born-again child of God is blessed. Don't stay there waiting for your blessing, receive your blessing by faith. It was released two thousand years ago. Whatever you have not seen in your life yet is not God's fault because God has played His part, you are lagging behind in your part. You are not using the power given to you, and you are not using your faith to receive what has been given. Reach out for it. In the story of the prodigal son, the father said, "All I have is thine." All God has is yours already.

*Not rendering evil for evil, or railing for railing:
but contrariwise blessing; knowing that ye are thereunto called,
that ye should inherit a blessing.*
I Peter 3:9

Be conscious of why you were called. You were called to be blessed. You were called to inherit God's blessings. By the call of salvation, you have inherited the Father's blessing. It's a call into what has been done on your behalf. It's like a call into a banquet, a buffet where all things are ready. You don't have to work for it; you just have to pick whatever you want by faith.

*He that spared not his own Son, but delivered him up for us all,
how shall he not with him also freely give us all things?*
Romans 8:32

With the release of Jesus to you, all things were released into your life. If God did not spare His Son but freely gave Him to us, would He not freely given us all things as well? If Jesus was released, what is that blessing you are looking for that has not been released? Is it bigger than Jesus? God is not withholding any blessing from you. It is God's will that you have all things. He has given you all things by giving you Jesus Christ. He has finished His part. That's the greatest miracle. Every other miracle is hinged on this great miracle, the miracle of salvation. You did not pay anything for it. Why do you think you need to strive for the other things you need? Jesus Christ has met your needs. He is all you need to have all your needs met. Jesus was freely given, and all things were freely given to you through Him. Grace already blesses you.

*Then said he unto him, A certain man made a great supper, and
bade many: And sent his servant at supper time to say to them that
were bidden, Come; for all things are now ready.*
Luke 14:16-17

There is a banquet of blessing already waiting for you by grace. It is waiting for your faith response to receive. You have been called into abundant blessing. Everything is set. Grace makes you enjoy what you have not laboured for. All things are now ready by grace. You don't have to go shopping and go into the kitchen and start racking your brain on what to cook. No hassle, no hustle. It's enjoyment time. Faith is all you need to maximise the moment and take delivery of what has been prepared for you. Everything has been prepared. Food is ready! It will be out of place to go to a buffet and ask where you can wash the plates or what work you need to do. God is not interested in what you want to do; He wants you to enjoy what He has done. We like to do to get, but God is saying I have done it, receive it by faith. Command your blessings. We are in a great supper, a great buffet of grace where all manner of grace has been made available. What you believe for is what you get. Your work is the work of faith. You are not working to get God to do something. You are exercising your faith in what He has done.

> It's already done!
> You have been blessed.
> You have been healed.
> You have been delivered.
> You have been made prosperous.
> You have been made fruitful.
> You have been made a success.
> You have been favoured.
> You have been forgiven.
> You have been made righteous.
> It is done!

Let your faith stand in this understanding that everything is done already. Reach out for what has been done in your spirit and enjoy it. It's yours. All the Father has is thine! Faith doesn't beg to receive what has been given. Faith takes what has been given. Your faith is to receive what the finished work of Christ has given. Grace has gone to work, while faith is here to enjoy what grace has worked for.

> *Who his own self bare our sins in his own body on the tree,*
> *that we, being dead to sins, should live unto righteousness:*
> *by whose stripes ye were healed.*
> I PETER 2:24

His stripes healed us. It's done. It happened two thousand years ago. It's not what He is going to do. It's what He has done already. You don't have sickness and disease in your redeemed spirit. It's not possible. Your spirit is perfect, and it's above sickness and disease. That's why you have to draw out what has been done in your spirit to the physical realm by faith. If you are sick in your body, speak to it to conform to the real you. You are not the sick trying to get healed; you are the healed who the devil is trying to make sick. By His stripes, you are already healed. You have to fight that sickness. The spirit of a man will sustain his infirmity (Proverb 18:14). Your spirit has what it takes to uphold from body. That's what it means to fight the good fight of faith. There is no sickness in the real you. Your spirit man has been healed. Say what you want to see in your body. What has been taken has been taken, it's no longer there. Sickness is not in your spirit, and therefore it's not permitted to be in your body. Put your hands on wherever you are having discomfort, speak to it with this understanding. Command it to go in the name of Jesus. I command every sickness and disease to leave your body right now in Jesus name. Amen!

> *But if the Spirit of him that raised up Jesus from the dead dwell in*
> *you, he that raised up Christ from the dead shall also quicken your*
> *mortal bodies by his Spirit that dwelleth in you.*
> ROMANS 8:11

If the Spirit of God that raised up Christ from the dead dwells in you, He that raised up Christ from the dead shall also quicken your mortal bodies by His Spirit that dwells in you. You are born again. The Holy Spirit dwells in you, and He is a life-giving Spirit. He quickens to life every deadness. He gives life to everything called dead in your body. Sicknesses and diseases are part of death. Death is more than just lifelessness. It is everything that has to do with misfortunes, failures, diseases, sicknesses, retrogression, unfruitfulness and depression. Everything that does not give glory to God is tagged dead. You have the power of life in you. Your body needs to know that you know what your spirit carries. The devil needs to know that you know. Address it; it has no place in your body because the quickening power of the Holy Spirit is in your spirit. Use what you have to get what you want.

That it might be fulfilled which was spoken by Esaias the prophet, saying, Himself took our infirmities, and bare our sicknesses.
MATTHEW 8:17

This was a quote from prophet Isaiah prophesying about Jesus saying, "Himself took our infirmities, and bore our sicknesses." He was not talking about healing that took place somewhere else; he was talking about healing that took place in your spirit. What has been done in your spirit is meant to reflect in the physical. He took it long ago before that symptom came. Before that disease afflicted you, it has been taken care of. That sickness and disease you find in your body now is a mirage. Speak to it. The real deal is that your infirmities have been taken (past tense) and He has borne your sicknesses. You don't actually have them. Your spirit has been healed, don't accept what the devil throws at you. Repel it by the power of the grace of God in your spirit. Cast out every spirit of infirmity militating against your body in the name of Jesus. When you pray, always pray from a blessed angle. You are praying to see your blessings in the physical, but it has been released in the spiritual.

TAKE AWAY DECLARATIONS

Thank you, Lord, you are the source of my blessing.

Father, I choose blessing by walking in your covenant.

Father, I command your blessing upon my life to be evident for all to see in Jesus name.

Father, let the blessings of Abraham upon my life begin to speak (Galatians 3:13-14)

Father, let me be satisfied with favour and let me be full of your blessing like Naphtali (Deuteronomy 33:23)

I reap a hundredfold harvest like Isaac in the name of Jesus (Genesis 26:12)

I am blessed like Jacob (Genesis 28:1)

My baskets and store are blessed (Deuteronomy 28:5)

I am favoured like Nehemiah to finish the assignment God has given me in Jesus name (Nehemiah 2:5)

Lord, I put first your kingdom and your righteousness, and all things are added to me.

My going out and coming in is blessed in Jesus name

I am blessed in the city and blessed in the field

I command your blessing on my storehouse.

Everything my hand touches is blessed in Jesus name.

By the stripes of Jesus, I am healed. He took my sickness; He carried my pain. I believe it is the will of God for me to be healed. I am healed in Jesus name.

I break every curse of infirmity, sickness, premature death and diseases off my body in the name of Jesus.

I break every curse of witchcraft and destruction over my body from both sides of my family in the name of Jesus.

In the name of Jesus, I speak to every sickness in my body, and I command it to leave.

PRE-CHAPTER POEM
Born to Reign

We are born to win; We are born to reign in life, we are born-again as a victor, not a victim.

We were born with all it takes to reign over Satan, sin, the world and the flesh. We're not merely human; We're Superman human. The Spirit of the Lord dwells in us. We have the power of God in us. We're too loaded to fail. We have been equipped with what it will take to live a triumphant life. We're not designed for failure; We're designed for success.

We're born to win; We're born to reign in life, We're born-again as a victor, not a victim.

We know who we are. We know where we came from and we know where we're going. We got our father's DNA. God is our father. He is the King of kings, and He has made us kings to rule and reign in this life. We have no business being ruled over. We're in charge here. The devil has no place in us. We have been given an abundance of grace and the gift of righteousness to rule and reign over life's circumstances. We're not designed for defeat; We're designed for victory.

We're born to win; We're born to reign in life, We're born-again as a victor, not a victim.

Chapter 8
REIGNING IN LIFE BY ABUNDANCE OF GRACE

It is God's desire that we reign in this life till Jesus returns. Just as battles are inevitable as a Christian, so are ruling and reigning over these battles inevitable. If you don't take responsibility to rule, you will be ruled out. Many things are out there to derail your destiny, it takes ruling and reigning by abundant grace to succeed over them. You have been empowered by grace to win in every facet of life. It is God's mandate for you to reign over life's circumstances. God has authorised you to reign in this life. Grace is a supernatural power for reigning in life. Abundance of grace is what you need to reign over the devil, sin, the world, and the flesh. God's will is that whatever we face in this life we experience victory over it. We are not designed for failure; we are designed for success. We are not designed for defeat; we are designed for victory. We are designed to be overcomers in Christ Jesus. That's our reality. That's who we are. We don't fight to lose; we fight to win. We are fighting from a winner's standpoint. God created Adam for dominion. He was meant to rule and reign on earth, but he lost his dominion to Satan. Obviously, God had a plan B to restore man to the place of dominion. His original intent was to see man in dominion. Jesus came to reinstate man back to the place of dominion.

> *And from Jesus Christ, who is the faithful witness, and the first begotten of the dead, and the prince of the kings of the earth. Unto him that loved us, and washed us from our sins in his own blood, And hath made us kings and priests unto God and his Father; to him be glory and dominion for ever and ever. Amen.*
> REVELATION 1:5-6

We have been made kings and priests to rule and reign on the earth until Jesus returns. We have no business been ruled over by things we should be ruling. The lost dominion has been reinstated. We are no longer slaves to anything; we are now kings and priests. We are in a higher kingdom and meant reign over the kingdom of darkness, sin, the world, and the flesh. We are in charge on earth. We have been empowered by grace to rule. Let's exercise our authority in ruling and reigning. Kings rule and princes decree justice (Proverbs 8:15).

> *And hast made us unto our God kings and priests: and we shall reign on the earth.*
> REVELATION 5:10

It's high time we started using our authority. We have been authorised and sponsored by grace to reign on earth. You are a king and priest. Kings reign and rule. You must take dominion over the world, over the devil, over sin, and over your flesh. Let's look at what it takes to rule and how to rule.

> *For if by one man's offence death reigned by one; much more they which receive abundance of grace and of the gift of righteousness shall reign in life by one, Jesus Christ.)*
> ROMANS 5:17

For by the offence of one man (Adam) death reigned, much more as we have received abundance of grace and the gift of righteousness we shall also reign in life by one Jesus Christ. The abundance of grace, the gift of righteousness and one Jesus Christ are all summed up in grace. Remember that Grace is God's Reliable Abundance by Christ's Effort. Jesus was the epitome of God's supernatural grace. He brought an abundance of grace our way. The gift of righteousness is a subset of the abundance of God's grace. It's one of the diverse by-products of this great grace.

In Adam death reigned through sin. The sin Adam committed brought death (Romans 5:12), but by Jesus' obedience to go to the cross, there was a release of an abundance of grace for us to reign now through faith. Death connotes poverty, sickness, disease, failure, retrogression, and all oppressions of the devil. Whatever does not give glory to God is death. Sin and death ruled and reigned over us in Adam, but the good news is that Jesus paid a huge price to get us out of sin and death. We have been set free and have been given an abundance of grace and the gift of righteousness which is a by-product of grace to reign in this life. Grace has saved us and has empowered us to reign in this life. Every born-again child of God has received an abundance of grace to reign over Satan, sin, the world, and the flesh. You cannot reign without grace. Grace is the work of the cross, and it is God's power for you to reign in life.

RULING AND REIGNING BY IDENTIFYING WITH WHAT JESUS DID

And they overcame him by the blood of the Lamb, and by the word of their testimony; and they loved not their lives unto the death.
REVELATION 12:11

They overcome the devil by

a) the blood of the Lamb,

b) by the word of their testimonies and

c) they loved not their lives unto death.

Overcoming by the blood of the Lamb: You reign over the devil by the blood of the lamb. You need to use the blood to fight against anything militating against your life. The blood is for you to enforce your victory over that challenge. Address it by the blood of Jesus. Decree that whatever is contrary to what the blood has been shed for should be destroyed. Because the blood has been shed to remove any obstacle, the blood of Jesus is against that issue of concern in your life in the name of Jesus. When you are faced with challenges, speak the blood of Jesus.

> *In whom we have redemption through his blood, the forgiveness of sins, according to the riches of his grace;*
> EPHESIANS 1:7

Your redemption was established by the shedding of the blood. You are redeemed from that challenge already, just bring the problem under subjection by the blood.

> *How much more shall the blood of Christ, who through the eternal Spirit offered himself without spot to God, purge your conscience from dead works to serve the living God?*
> HEBREWS 9:14

How much more shall the blood of Christ, who through the eternal Spirit offered Himself without spot to God, purge your conscience from dead works to serve the living God?

The blood has been shed to purge your conscience from every dead work so that you can serve the living God. Sin is a dead work; you have to address it with the blood of Jesus. Don't sit and watch sin take over when you have been empowered by the blood to take over. You need to stop everything trying to stop you from serving the living God. The blood has done it, use it. The blood has fixed it, exercise your freedom.

Overcoming by the word of your testimonies: You have great testimonies in Christ, testimonies of your new reality and the great things He has done for you. The word of your testimonies needs to agree with what Jesus did for you. You need to identify with it. It is time to put your faith into practice. Identify with what happened on the cross by faith.

> *Now the just shall live by faith: but if any man draw back, my soul shall have no pleasure in him.*
> HEBREWS 10:38

You are living by faith. Don't accept defeat. Don't talk failure. Don't accept whatever the devil is throwing at you. For instance, the devil makes you feel like you can't live a righteous life. Sometimes you end up speaking to yourself negatively. After listening to the lies of the devil, you say something like, "Maybe I just can't live it, maybe I'm flawed. I don't know how to stop this sin. I find myself doing what I don't want to do. I have messed up, I can't be good, I can't continue anymore. I give up, I'm tired. God is not happy with me and doesn't love me because of this sin. I have disappointed God and He has given up on me. Let me just live in this mess, that's me, no good thing in me." All lies of the devil!

You need to start speaking the word of your testimonies to yourself. "I am the righteousness of God in Christ Jesus. Though I mess up, that's not me. The real me is righteous and truly holy. God loves me; He has made me righteous and truly holy. He has forgiven me of my past, present and future sins. I have been made perfect in my spirit. I have God's ability in me to live a righteous life. I'm empowered by grace to live above sin. Christ dwells in me. If Jesus cannot live in sin, I cannot live in sin."

Faith speaks. You must declare what God has done for you, not what the devil has done to you. God has given you the gift of righteousness to reign in life. He loves you with an everlasting love. God will never give up on you. Though He hates what you did, He loves you. You are the apple of His eye. With this understanding, when you fail now, you know that it is not you. You just did stupid stuff, that's not who you truly are. You step up and step out of your mess. You are a victor.

> *That the communication of thy faith may become effectual by the acknowledging of every good thing which is in you in Christ Jesus.*
> PHILEMON 1:6

Your faith does not keep quiet. Faith communicates. It speaks. Let the communication of your faith be effectual in acknowledging every good thing which is in you in Christ. Whatever has been done in you, speak it. The effectiveness of your faith is in your declaration. You must keep talking about it to see it. You have been perfected in your spirit. Christ has done good things in you. Profess it to live it. Don't accept what you are not by keeping quiet. React against whatever is against the real you. Every good thing you desire to do has been done in you. Talk about every good thing He has done inside you to see the manifestation on the outside.

> *For a just man falleth seven times, and riseth up again: but the wicked shall fall into mischief.*
> PROVERBS 24:16

With this understanding, when you fall, you don't remain in your fallen state. You repent and rise up. Don't settle for what the devil is saying to you. You have been given supernatural strength by grace to conquer. Speak the Scriptures: "I can do all things through Christ who strengtheneth me." That's grace. Inner strength is given to you to live in the face of challenges. Receive grace to stand in Jesus name.

Overcoming by not holding on to your life: They love not their lives unto death. Don't still say, "This is my life." It's no longer your life. It's the very life of God. You no longer exist; Christ is living in you now. Live your life for Him totally. Don't continue to hold on to your life. Are you committed unto death to live your life for Jesus? The way you overcome is by not loving your life, even unto death. Do you love Jesus more than anything? If you are going to reign, you must have passion for Jesus. You have to give up things for the sake of your love for Christ. Give up your life so He can walk in you and through you. Don't say,

"This is my life, I do whatever I want to do with it." It's not your life anymore; you need to yield yourself to Him.

> *For the love of Christ constraineth us; because we thus judge, that if one died for all, then were all dead: And that he died for all, that they which live should not henceforth live unto themselves, but unto him which died for them, and rose again.*
> II CORINTHIANS 5:14-15

The love of Christ puts restrictions on you. It puts you in check. The love of Christ confines you. You don't want to hurt His feelings. Love is a constrainer, put Christ first in your priorities. Before you think of anything, you think of Him. You don't see it as your life but His life. You see yourself dead already in Him. Now you don't live unto yourself but unto Him. If it was your life, you could live it the way you want. But because it's no longer yours, you need to live it the way He wants. This happens by you not loving your life, even unto death. You can do anything for love. Your passion for Christ can keep you away from sin. Your love can make you rule and reign in this life because you will be love-motivated in what you do. We are no longer alive; we are all dead. We should recognise that the life we live now we live by faith. It is not ours; it's His life. We must live it for Him. An understanding of this builds a consciousness of your new reality in you. You don't hold onto your opinions about things, but instead adopt His opinions.

> *I am crucified with Christ: nevertheless I live; yet not I, but Christ liveth in me: and the life which I now live in the flesh I live by the faith of the Son of God, who loved me, and gave himself for me.*
> GALATIANS 2:20

Identify that this life you are living now is no longer yours. You are living by faith. Christ lives in you. When He died, you died, and when He resurrected, you resurrected. You are living for Him now by faith. Every born-again Christian lives by faith and not by sight (II Corinthians 5:7). You don't operate in the five senses. You operate by your spiritual senses. There is a war going on the inside of you: Your spirit wants to do what's right; your flesh fights against your spirit. Your spirit has been victorious. Christ has made you victorious in your spirit, but your flesh is contesting that victory. You are an overcomer already by faith.

> *For this is the love of God, that we keep his commandments: and his commandments are not grievous. For whatsoever is born of God overcometh the world: and this is the victory that overcometh the world, even our faith.*
> I JOHN 5:3-4

Our ruling and reigning are by faith in what has been done. You have to believe it and identify with it. Believe you have been dead and that settles it. A dead man in the graveyard cannot sin. The life you live now you live by the faith in Jesus Christ who loved you and gave Himself for you. You are now living for Him by faith. Christ in you has placed you in dominion over every challenge in life. Faith makes you a world overcomer. When your obedience stems from your love for God, His commandments are not grievous. You delight in obeying Him. The commandments of God are only grievous if you are doing something so that God will love you, if you are doing things out of the law instead of out of love. If you are doing something to be accepted and blessed, it becomes grievous. But if you know you have been loved and accepted in Jesus the Beloved, obeying God becomes a delight.

UNDERSTANDING THE PROCESS OF RULING AND REIGNING

There is a process involved to rule and reign. If you want to rule and reign you can't dodge the process. There is a process that must be followed to get to the throne where you rule and reign. It has been done already, that's God's design for you, but you need to align with what has been done. You must understand this process and identify with it. Your ruling comes out of your relationship with the Lord. You have to learn this process and appropriate it in your life.

Here is the process: Jesus was crucified with you, died, buried, raised and you are seated and reigning in this life with Him. This process is not a day process. It's a daily process. You have to walk by faith every day in this process. You have to know how you were connected to His crucifixion, death, burial, resurrection and how you are reigning with Him now. Not that He is reigning without you, He is reigning with you. When Jesus was crucified, we were crucified. When He died, we died. When He was buried, we were buried. When He was raised, we were raised, and now we are seated with Him and reigning with Him.

Most of the time, we say Jesus was crucified, but we skip the important part that we were crucified with Him. He did not die for Himself; He died for and with you.

> *And that he died for all, that they which live should not henceforth live unto themselves, but unto him which died for them, and rose again. Wherefore henceforth know we no man after the flesh: yea, though we have known Christ after the flesh, yet now henceforth know we him no more. Therefore if any man be in Christ, he is a new creature: old things are passed away; behold, all things are become new.*
> II CORINTHIANS 5:15-17

There was an old creature, and there is a new creature. There was a part of you that passed away with the death of Jesus on the cross. You become a new creature completely in your spirit. Who you were in Adam died and was crucified. That part of you that was an alcoholic, fornicator, homosexual, lesbian, backbiter, liar, masturbator, addict to pornography was crucified on the cross. That old you was dealt with on the Cross. You are dead already. A new you has emerged in Christ. A new species. You are living now just like you have not existed before. All things have been made new in Christ. You may struggle with your past, struggle with your flesh, but that does not define you. Walk in the Spirit so that you don't fulfil the desires of the flesh. Identify with the new you, not the old you.

> *I am crucified with Christ: nevertheless I live; yet not I, but Christ liveth in me: and the life which I now live in the flesh I live by the faith of the Son of God, who loved me, and gave himself for me.*
> GALATIANS 2:20

Repeat this Scripture to yourself often. It's in professing who you are by faith that you walk in the reality of what Christ has done. When you see yourself doing something contrary to the real you in Christ, speak to it. Say what Christ has done for you on the cross. He crucified you on the cross: "I lost the old me on the cross, and the new is in union with Christ. Christ lives in me and the life I live now, I live by faith." You are practically living in adherence to and reliance on the Son of God that gave Himself for you.

Let me ask you this question: If the very life of Christ lives in you, do you think that life can overcome pornography, drugs, fornication, lying, smoking, stealing, backbiting, and adultery? You need to have faith and mix faith with these things. Jesus came to set you free. He came to empower you. You can do all things now through Christ who strengthens you. God lives, rules and reigns in you now. My new life is in Christ. With this understanding, you can now overcome the world and sin. You shared in Jesus' crucifixion. Whenever what has been dead wants to surface in your body, you will be able to address it. The dead don't struggle with challenges; you are dead to sin by faith. See yourself as the dead who is now living a new life by faith in Jesus' finished work.

> *Knowing this, that our old man is crucified with him, that the body of sin might be destroyed, that henceforth we should not serve sin. For he that is dead is freed from sin.*
> ROMANS 6:6-7

We have been crucified, and the body of sin has been destroyed on the cross. It takes faith to walk in this reality. That's what Christ has done for you and with you on the cross. It is not God's will for anything to enslave you. Don't permit anything to enslave you. The body of sin has been killed. You must know that you have been dead with Christ and are dead to sin. You don't have to serve sin anymore, you have been freed from sin. Death frees you from sin. If you are in doubt, go to the cemetery and stay there for a week to see if there is any practice of sin.

Faith is your now reality in what has been finished by Christ Jesus. Believing in His finished work, the proof of your faith shows when you can totally use it to align with the finished work of Christ.

Moreover the law entered, that the offence might abound. But where sin abounded, grace did much more abound:
ROMANS 5:20

Sin is more than just an immoral act; it's a power. It is a satanic influence that entices you to do things against your spiritual will. When you yield to sin, it enslaves you, it destroys you and makes you live less than what God has ordained you to be. Glory to God for grace. But where sin abounds, grace did much more abound. God's grace is more abundant to overcome sin. Grace is God's supernatural design to empower you against this body of sin that has been crucified. It takes the power of God to break every addiction. That power has been released already. Your dominion lies in knowing these things. Mixing faith with grace makes you live supernaturally above sin. Grace is a divine resistance against every sin. Various addictions ensnare many, but the good news is that Jesus can break it away from you. That yoke is broken right now in Jesus name.

Death: we are freed from sin by death (Romans 6:7). Death breaks the power of sin. Death releases you from sin, the death of who you used to be, how you were in Adam. You need to mix faith with these things. It's all by faith. You were not there when it happened; you believe in it now to see the reality of what was done. That's faith. When it took place, you were there in the spirit. It's time to live out the life that was released through the cross.

> *God forbid. How shall we, that are dead to sin,*
> *live any longer therein?*
> ROMANS 6:2

You have been dead to sin. How shall we that are dead to sin live any longer therein? We don't stay in sin. We must reckon ourselves by faith to be truly dead to sin.

> *Likewise reckon ye also yourselves to be dead indeed unto sin,*
> *but alive unto God through Jesus Christ our Lord.*
> ROMANS 6:11

You have to consider yourself as a dead man to sin. You need to believe that you no longer exist, the you that used to sin is dead already. You are alive unto God through Jesus Christ our Lord. Your new life is living; your old life is dead. In Jesus, God destroyed your old man.
By the grace of God, you can overcome that temptation. Your confession of faith is this: I used to be that, I am not that anymore, my old man is dead. I'm a new creature. A brand-new being. A new species. That's not my nature anymore. I have a righteous nature.   Use your faith now to celebrate in your crucifixion, death, burial and resurrection of Jesus. Put yourself in the picture. Because you were truly there by faith. By faith all He went through, He went through with you. Say, "Father by faith I reckon myself dead to alcohol, pornography, fornication, stealing and _____." Just name whatever it is.

Burial: Baptised into His death, immersed, submerged, to break the power of sin. When you got born again the Holy Spirit baptised you into the body of Christ. Spiritually there was a baptism that took place in you at new birth that gave birth to the new you (1 Corinthians 12:13). Baptism by water is a physical identification with what has been done spiritually. You have reckoned yourself as one that has been buried in Him.

> *Therefore we are buried with him by baptism into death: that like as Christ was raised up from the dead by the glory of the Father, even so we also should walk in newness of life.*
> ROMANS 6:4

You have been buried with Jesus by baptism into death. Through His death, the power of your sinful nature was shattered. Your sin-loving nature was buried with Him by baptism when He died, when God the Father with His glorious power brought Him back to life, you were given His wonderful new life to enjoy.

RAISED AND REIGNING WITH HIM

If you then be risen with Christ (Colossians 3:1), not that you are going to rise, it means it has been done already. You should seek things above. Be spiritually minded.

> *Now if we be dead with Christ, we believe that we shall also live with him: Knowing that Christ being raised from the dead dieth no more; death hath no more dominion over him.*
> ROMANS 6:8-9

If you were dead with Him, you are alive with Him now, ruling and reigning with Him. Death had no dominion over Him, and He lives in you, so death has no dominion over you. You are in charge now. You have been raised from the dead to dominate your world, not to be dominated.

> *And hath raised us up together, and made us sit together in heavenly places in Christ Jesus:*
> EPHESIANS 2:6

When Jesus was resurrected, we were resurrected, and now we are sitting with Him. We are ruling and reigning with Him. By faith, I reckon myself dead to sin and alive unto God.

UNDERSTANDING THE WAR BETWEEN YOUR SPIRIT AND FLESH

There is a war between the spirit and flesh.

> *For that which I do I allow not: for what I would, that do I not; but what I hate, that do I. If then I do that which I would not, I consent unto the law that it is good. Now then it is no more I that do it, but sin that dwelleth in me.*
> ROMANS 7:15-17

There are times you find yourself doing things you never wanted to do. You hate what you do, but still, you do it. No longer I that do it but sin that dwells in me. It is sin that is working in me. There is no good thing in the flesh. You need to learn how to walk with Jesus, to live by faith. In the Scripture above, Paul is trying to say that if he tries to live this Christian life after the flesh, he will fail and fall every time. He can't rely on his flesh. It will always bring failure.

There is combat between the flesh and the spirit. Your five senses are not dependable; you will fail and fall if you rely on your senses. No more I that do it but sin that dwells in me says Paul. Say to yourself; I am a new creature, I renounce that, I repent of that, I will follow God. It is not me doing that sin, that's not the real me. That's the old me. This is not to say that you should not be accountable for what you have done but that you need to take responsibility not to live in it. You need to turn. Sin has consequences. You may be a Christian with weaknesses, but that's not who you are. You need to get up and repent. Learn to walk in the spirit, not after the flesh. Walking after the flesh will produce hatred, anger, lying, fornication, and malice. Each time you find yourself in any form of mess, that's not you, that's your member fighting you. Your flesh is at work.

> *O wretched man that I am! who shall deliver me*
> *from the body of this death?*
> *I thank God through Jesus Christ our Lord. So then with the mind*
> *I myself serve the law of God; but with the flesh the law of sin.*
> ROMANS 7:24-25

Paul was basically asking, "Who shall deliver me from this body of death? I thank God for Jesus. Through Jesus, I have been delivered." Whom the son sets free is free indeed (John 8:38). Jesus is your new way of living. Jesus did not just come to improve your life; He came to be your very life. You are living as Jesus. He lives in you. Without Him in you, you can do nothing. Once you understand who Christ has made you to be, you can start appropriating the grace of God. You have been freed from the nature of sin. Get out of Adam and get into Christ. Take cover in Christ Jesus. Jesus is the solution. He has done it.

> *There is therefore now no condemnation to them which are in*
> *Christ Jesus, who walk not after the flesh, but after the Spirit.*
> ROMANS 8:1

We do not walk after the flesh any longer, but after the spirit. In Christ, there is no condemnation. Why? When you sin, God says, "That's not you." Get it right. God has forgiven you already. You have been loved. You need to repent and walk after the spirit. The law could not make you righteous. We have been made the righteousness of Christ. We have to learn to walk after the spirit. Your repentance and confession of your sins are not to get God to love you; you don't do it to get God to save you. You have been loved, and you have been saved already. You just need to repent, knowing that the sin is not you. The real you wants to do right. Respond to what's real and do right. Don't dwell on your mistakes as a lifestyle. You can't please and serve God in the flesh. Live in the spirit.

What does it mean to be carnal? It means to be ruled by the five senses, to be driven by your five senses. A carnal person is circular, not spiritual. Carnal means flesh, meat, skin, circular or worldly. Merely human. You wait to see it to believe it. You are being carnal if you walk with feelings. Your feelings are not true reflections of the truth. Your feelings can be manipulated. They that are in the flesh cannot please God. If you are truly born again, you are not in the flesh. You are in the spirit, the Spirit of God dwells in you. Your spirit is the righteousness of God. You are different in the spirit.

For they that are after the flesh do mind the things of the flesh; but they that are after the Spirit the things of the Spirit.
ROMANS 8:5

Those after the flesh are controlled by their own desires. Their flesh influences them. They set their minds on the things of the flesh, things which gratify the flesh. But they that are under the influence of the Spirit will always mind the things of the Spirit. Just the way the flesh lures you to do things contrary to your spirit, so also allow your spirit to lead you in all ways to do things contrary to the flesh. Walk against the influence of the flesh by walking in the spirit. To be carnally minded is death but to be spiritually minded is life and peace (Romans 8:6). The spirit realm and physical world don't mix. You are a spirit that has a soul and lives in a body. Spirit, mind, and body. If you have given your life to Christ, your spirit is born again, righteous and truly holy. Your mind is a mediator, the middle man between your spirit and flesh. It negotiates to be in agreement with any of the parties between your spirit and flesh, depending on what it's exposed to. Your mind is either being renewed to agree with the spirit to override the flesh, or your mind think on the flesh, look at the flesh, is dominated by the flesh which then overrides the spirit. Your body (flesh) is not born again. It's susceptible to temptations and attacks. It is important to set your mind on God for your spirit to dominate your life. Be controlled by the desires of the spirit, not the desires of the flesh. Retrain your mind. Fix your mind on the things above. Your flesh and your spirit are at war with one another. They don't mix. They are parallel to each other. They are against each other. The mind determines the winning party each time. It's neutral on its own. It only works with what you set it on. What you put into the mind determines what side it should take in the battle. It takes the side of the spirit when spiritual things are inputed into it and takes the side of the flesh when fleshly things are dominating it. You are either in the spirit or you are in the flesh. Let your mind be spiritually minded. The carnal way of thinking will produce a carnal result, and spiritual way of thinking will produce spiritual results. The carnal way of thinking about sex can destroy you, but there is a spiritual way of thinking. You can't think the way you used to think before you got born again and expect a different result. If you think like those in the world, and you want to live differently, it won't be possible. If you desire to be different, it must be complete. You must think differently. Your mind must be renewed and you have to keep renewing your mind every day to undergo the transformation process that God wants you to undergo to get the kind of results you desire (Romans 12:3). If you are not willing to renew your mind, you can't experience victory. Renewing your mind is a process you have to do to experience change in your life. Don't ignore it.

> *This I say then, Walk in the Spirit, and ye shall not fulfil the lust of the flesh. For the flesh lusteth against the Spirit, and the Spirit against the flesh: and these are contrary the one to the other: so that ye cannot do the things that ye would.*
> GALATIANS 5:16-17

We are admonished to walk in the spirit so that we don't fulfil the lust of the flesh. He did not say the flesh will stop lusting against the spirit. Flesh is always an issue. The war against the flesh is a consistent war, but you keep getting better. You need to make the flesh decrease for the spirit to increase. You need to walk after the spirit so that you don't fulfil the lust of the flesh. The Holy Spirit is working in you and causing you to reign in life by Jesus Christ. Your reigning over sin is by grace. There is a constant battle between your flesh and your spirit. Without Jesus, you can do nothing. You cannot overcome the weakness of the flesh independent of walking in the spirit. It takes the grace of God to become victorious. The only way to crucify the deeds of the flesh is to walk in the spirit. Put no confidence in the flesh, but in the spirit. When you walk in the spirit, your flesh does not keep lusting.

What does it mean to walk in the spirit? It means you are being led by the Holy Spirit in whatever you do. It means you are walking in accordance with who you truly are in Christ. There is a new you in Christ. You have to recognise that and walking in the spirit means you are now responding to the new you by the help of the Holy Spirit. Who you are in the spirit is vital to your walk in the spirit. We know in the spirit we are the righteousness of God. We are joint heirs with Christ. We are new creatures. We are the body of Christ. We are blessed in the spirit. We are lifted. We are the head and not the tail, above only and never beneath. We are healed. We are strengthened with might in our inner man. We can choose to walk after the spirit versus walking after the flesh. The flesh is always parallel to what the spirit says we are. The flesh will bring you depression, discouragement, diseases, and weakness. You have to fight those things by faith because they are not in your spirit. When you walk in the spirit, your focus should be on the spirit and not the flesh. You have a new focus. It's a spirit-centred focus on the promises of God, not on the problems you are facing. Your eyes should be fixed on the promises and you should proclaim the promises instead of talking about the problems. It means you are relying on the grace of God to live a victorious life. You are focusing on the promises instead of the law (Romans 6:14), and not allowing sin to have its way. Trying to figure out a rule or regulation to get out of sin strengthens sin. Anything besides the grace of our Lord Jesus Christ gives power to sin and brings you under the law. Walking in the spirit also means you are looking unto Jesus as the author and the finisher of your faith, not looking unto yourself and what you can offer, instead looking unto the one that has done a finished work on your behalf. You are walking by faith in what He has done versus walking by sight. Walking by sight brings you into natural living but walking by faith puts you perpetually in the supernatural.

CONFESSING YOUR FAITH

To trust and yield to God, faith speaks the answer, not the problem.

> *That the communication of thy faith may become effectual by the acknowledging of every good thing which is in you in Christ Jesus.*
> PHILEMON 1:6

Your faith does not keep quiet. Faith communicates. It speaks. Let the communication of your faith be effectual in acknowledging every good thing which is in you in Christ, not the bad things happening around you, not the bad choices or mistakes you made yesterday. Whatever has been done in you, speak it. The effectiveness of your faith is in your declaration. You must keep talking about it to see it. You have been perfected in your spirit. Christ has done good things in you. Profess it to live it. Don't accept what you are not by keeping quiet. React against whatever is against the real you. That's how you walk in the spirit, aligning with what has been done in your spirit man. Say what God has said, let God be true, and every other thing be a liar (Romans 3:4). Speak to every mountain (Mark 11:23-24). You allow your problem to talk to you, instead of talking to your problem. It takes the violent to prevail. The violent taketh it by force. You are triumphant in Christ. Faith says I am a new creature, not who I used to be. You have a challenge, don't allow that challenge to have you. Blessed is she that believes and has not yet seen, for there shall be a performance of the things which were told her from the lord (Luke 1:45). Faith believes what he can't see, to see it. Faith believes in God and speaks into reality all that God has done. Walk in the spirit, walk after the leading of the Holy Spirit.

WALKING AFTER THE SPIRIT

How do you walk after the Spirit?

> *For they that are after the flesh do mind the things of the flesh; but they that are after the Spirit the things of the Spirit. For to be carnally minded is death; but to be spiritually minded is life and peace.*
> ROMANS 8:5-6

You have to set your mind on the things that gratify the spirit. Your mind can be either carnally minded or spiritually minded. It cannot be neutral. Your mind can operate in the spirit as well as in the physical. The spirit and the flesh are contrary one to another; they walk against each other. In my spirit, I am united with Christ. In my flesh, I am helpless and hopeless. There is nothing good in my flesh, but everything has been made good in my spirit. Your spirit is the eternal you, it will return to heaven from whence it came, while the flesh will go to the dust where it came from. There is an eternal you and a temporary you. If you mind the things of the Spirit, your life will be dominated with God's goodness, which guarantees life and peace. Learn to think after the spirit.

You have to renew your mind. It's a daily thing. You have to be accountable for your thought life. What do you think on often? What occupies your mind the most? Death means all that encompasses death and darkness, depression, confusion, sickness, diseases, every work of the flesh, etc. Whenever your mind deviates from thinking of Jesus, you start experiencing death of various kinds. Keep your mind on God. Stay in the spirit. Walk after the Spirit.

To be spiritually minded is to be dominated with truth, love, and faith. Spirit-mindedness also means to be word-minded (John 6:63). The Word of God is spirit. Meditate on God's goodness. Fasting and prayer also help to respond to the real you, which is your spirit man. It makes your spirit sensitive to the leading of God's Spirit. You can't be a man of the spirit and be a man of sin. Spirituality is the cure for carnality. Pay attention to your spirit.

TAKE AWAY DECLARATIONS

I am a son of God because I have faith in Christ Jesus and my faith is alive (Galatians 3:26, James 2:17)

I walk by faith and not by sight (II Corinthians 5:7)

I am the righteousness of God in Christ Jesus by faith (II Corinthians 5:21)

I am justified by my faith in Jesus (Romans 3:26)

The righteousness of God is revealed to me through faith in Jesus (Romans 3:22)

I am born again; I am righteous and truly holy.

I am who God says I am. I am the redeemed of the Lord. I'm a new species in Christ. I am a victor, not a victim of circumstances.

I am ruling and reigning over the devil, sin, the world and the flesh by abundance of grace and the gift of righteousness (Romans 5:17)

I do not walk according to the flesh but according to the Spirit (Romans 8:4)

I am made righteous by Christ Jesus, and I also practice righteousness because I'm born of God (I John 2:29)

I have been crucified with Christ, though I live, the old me no longer exist, but Christ lives in me now, and the real life I now have within this body is as a result of my faith in the Son of God, who loved me and gave Himself for me (Galatians 2:20)

What Christ did on the cross, He did with me. When He died, I died, when He was buried, I was buried, and when He was raised by the power of the Holy Ghost, I was raised. He is ruling and reigning, I am ruling and reigning with Him.

I reckon myself dead to sin but alive unto God through Jesus Christ our Lord (Romans 6:11)

PRE-CHAPTER POEM
Grace is My Strength

When I found grace, I found strength. I have inner fortitude to face challenges. I don't give up because grace is always there to pick me up when I fall down. I don't run away from challenges or allow myself to be defeated. I see each challenge as an opportunity to showcase grace. I fight with my inner strength when my outer strength fails. When my willpower can't help matters because it's limited, I turn to a most reliable power, which is the power of God's grace.

Grace is my strength in weakness.

I choose to focus on my strength. I can feed my strength; I can build my strength up. Enough of talking about my weakness, when I have the strength to outshine my weakness. I need to increase my strength. I am strong now because I have exercised my strength. I can be stronger. There is room for more improvement. I need to keep waxing strong in grace. I have found my strength it is called grace.

I can do all things through Christ who strengthens me. Jesus was grace personified. He lives in me and has given me grace over everything. I am empowered to excel. It's grace at work in me. I have this 'I can do all things' nature in me, the nature of Christ. There is no impossibility with me. Greater is He that is in me than he that is in the world. The greater one is in me. Greater power is in me.

Grace is my strength.

Chapter 9

BE STRONG IN GRACE

Thou therefore, my son, **be strong in the grace** *that is in Christ Jesus.*
II TIMOTHY 2:1

When Paul spoke to Timothy, he said, "My son, be strong in the grace that is in Christ Jesus." What he says to one, he says to all. Paul is telling us to be strong in the grace that is in Christ Jesus. Grace is more than just a concept; it is the power of God that gives you strength. Your strength determines what you can withstand. The stronger you are, the more you are capable of withstanding spiritual forces arrayed against your destiny. You need grace to be unyielding in the face of adversity. You have to be determined by grace to succeed over your challenges through faith. Grace does not give birth to weak people. No, grace gives birth to powerful, forceful people who are relentless, dogged, steadfast, and immovable in the face of challenges. There is a great supply of supernatural strength in God's grace to make you who God has ordained you to be. You have to be strong in this grace. One of the primary purposes of grace is to make you strong. You cannot be who God has called you to be without grace and cannot do what God has called you to do without grace. That's why Paul said you have to be strong in this grace. Grace is a strength needed for battle. You have been given grace, but you have to still grow in it by faith. You must increase your grace capacity.

> *Be sober, be vigilant; because your adversary the devil, as a roaring lion, walketh about, seeking whom he may devour:*
> *Whom resist stedfast in the faith, knowing that the same afflictions are accomplished in your brethren that are in the world.*
> *But the God of all grace, who hath called us unto his eternal glory by Christ Jesus, after that ye have suffered a while, make you perfect, stablish, strengthen, settle you.*
> I PETER 5:8-10

Know that you need to resist the devil steadfastly in faith. You don't have to faint; you don't have to give in and give out. You have to fight like a good soldier of Christ. You have been declared a victor already, but you still need to contend for victory and enforce your victory. You need to remain a defending champion as well. That challenge you face, that affliction you encounter, is common to man. It's not strange; it's not something you cannot succeed over. Grace has been released for your victory. Others have fought and have won. I have fought and won a battle against addiction. You too can take that battle to the battlefield with this understanding that you have what it takes. Go and destroy the enemies of your life and destiny. Giving up is not an option in this fight. Say to yourself that you have crossed the rubicon, there is no going back, you won't go back and can't go back to the way it used to be. You have come too far to allow this challenge to pull you down. You will fight with God's grace to get to your Promised Land. You have suffered for some time now. Every affliction that has gone on is terminated now in Jesus name.

The date permitted for you to experience a problem is *a while*, and anything beyond a while has exceeded its stay. It's time to be confrontational. It's time to use the weapon of God's grace. Whatever it is, speak to it. Speak to your mountain. Grace shows up on the scene to make you perfect, to establish you, to make you strong (strengthened) and to grant you all-around settlement. True grace will always make you stand strong (1 Peter 5:12). Grace is for you to stand firm.

PRIMARY PURPOSE OF GRACE

To make you perfect: Grace came to turn an imperfect you into a perfect you. If you are born again, you are perfect before God. Grace made you perfect. By God's grace, you have been declared without faults or mistakes in the sight of God. You are flawless. You don't have any reason to feel condemned for what you have done. You have been justified. To be justified means before God, you appear as one that has never done anything wrong. That's what God has done for you in Christ. See yourself the way God sees you and engage grace and faith to live a victorious life.

> *For by one offering he hath perfected for ever them that are sanctified.*
> HEBREWS 10:14

By the offering of Jesus, we have been perfected forever. Not that we are going to be perfect. We were made perfect. Maybe you realise in your mind that you still find imperfections in your member (body). I am not talking about your body, I am talking about your spirit. If you are born again, you have a perfected spirit. What you do in your body is not you. The real you has the real deal. It is a perfect spirit that is staying in that body. Your body is just housing the real you. You can't call your house *you*, your house is just where you stay. Your body is your earth suit, just the way we have spacesuits. It's what you need to live on the earth. When you make a mistake in your body, you don't accept it and continue to wallow in it. Tell your body to respond to the real you. Your body should start behaving according to who you are in your spirit by faith. You have to speak to it by faith that you have been made perfect and truly holy. When you do what you know is wrong, that's not you, that's not what you want to truly do. You only failed, but you are not a failure. You get up and get back on track. You repent of it and get it right with God, but that does not change that you have not been made perfect. It does not mean that God is mad at you, it does not mean that God does not love you any longer. God has already made you perfect in your spirit; He has loved you with an everlasting love, He has forgiven you already.

> *To the praise of the glory of his grace, wherein he hath made us accepted in the beloved.*
> EPHESIANS 1:6

You have been accepted. You don't have to pay for it. Somebody has paid for you to be reconciled back to God and that's Jesus Christ. He has made you accepted and perfected. You are one with Christ now. God sees you in Christ. You were accepted and made perfect in Christ. You are only made perfect in Christ.

To establish you: Another word for *stablish* is *establish*, it means to make you stable, firm and to set you up. Grace came with all the requirements needed to build you up and to put you in dignity.

> *The grace of our Lord Jesus Christ be with you all. Amen.*
> *Now to him that is of power to stablish you according to my gospel, and the preaching of Jesus Christ, according to the revelation of the mystery, which was kept secret since the world began,*
> ROMANS 16:24-25

This is the power of God's grace to establish you. Paul is saying that our Lord Jesus Christ has the power to establish you according to the Gospel, and we know that the Gospel of Paul was the Gospel of grace. It takes power for you to be established in the Word of Grace. Grace has appeared to everyone, but without a conscious expectation to grow and be established, you cannot get much from it. Grace has so much for you. You need to maximise it, for it is a good thing that the heart be established with grace (Hebrews 13:9). Let your heart be established by grace through faith in God's finished work as you study the Word of God so that you can be established in this life. He has done it all. You are only mixing your faith with what has been done, you have to discover it to enjoy it.

> *Now our Lord Jesus Christ himself, and God,*
> *even our Father, which hath loved us, and hath given us everlasting*
> *consolation and good hope through grace,*
> *Comfort your hearts, and stablish you in every good word and work.*
> II THESSALONIANS 2:16-17

Grace is here to establish you in every good word and work. It takes grace to speak the right word: an offence-free word, a soft word, a word in season. It takes grace to do the right work. Acceptable work. There is grace for service. There is giving grace. It takes the establishment of grace for you to exhibit good work. You are built up by grace unto good work. You bear righteous fruit by grace. You live a Holy life by grace.

> *For ye know the grace of our Lord Jesus Christ, that,*
> *though he was rich, yet for your sakes he became poor,*
> *that ye through his poverty might be rich.*
> II CORINTHIANS 8:9

Grace was released for your establishment in riches. It takes grace to make wealth. He became poor deliberately that we through His poverty might become rich. His grace entitled us to riches. We are established by grace to live in wealth now. We were impoverished in Adam, but in Christ, we are in a wealthy place. It's part of grace work for us to live in riches.

To make you strong (strengthen): Grace is your strength for living. It is your supernatural empowerment over the devil, this world, sin and the flesh.

> *For when we were yet without strength,*
> *in due time Christ died for the ungodly.*
> ROMANS 5:6

Christ died for us when we were weak, without strength. He died to give us strength. Amongst other things that were released to us was strength. Worthy is the Lamb that was slain to receive power, and riches, and wisdom, and strength, and honour, and glory, and blessing (Revelation 5:12). One of the things He received for us as part of our grace package was strength: strength to live above sin, strength to be in command, strength to live a victorious lifestyle and strength to fight any battle.

> *And I heard a loud voice saying in heaven, Now is come salvation, and strength, and the kingdom of our God, and the power of his Christ: for the accuser of our brethren is cast down, which accused them before our God day and night.*
> REVELATION 12:10

One of the things that accompanied salvation was strength. Without this supernatural strength, you cannot live this Christian life. Strength was released for you to excel. He did not just save you, He saved you and gave you the grace to become the victor He has made you to be. You must be strong in this grace. That's what you need to become all that God has planned in Christ for you to become.

> *And he said unto me, My grace is sufficient for thee: for my strength is made perfect in weakness. Most gladly therefore will I rather glory in my infirmities, that the power of Christ may rest upon me.*
> II CORINTHIANS 12:9

When you are weak in your flesh, you have the supernatural strength of God in your spirit man to draw from. You are not left without strength; you were not left helpless. The grace of God was given unto you. God did not say He would do it for you. He said He has given you what it takes to do it. "My grace is sufficient for you." My strength is made perfect in your weakness. Paul had to think twice to realise that he had it and started appropriating it, and that was the end of that challenge. You have what it takes, you have been given an inner fortitude to attack every challenge of life, and it is called grace. You can be very strong in this grace; you are no longer movable by anything the enemies throw at you.

> *Finally, my brethren, be strong in the Lord,*
> *and in the power of his might.*
> EPHESIANS 6:10

You have to be strong in the Lord and in the power of His might so that you can keep reigning and ruling in this life. Grace has to be on the increase in your life. Grace is the power of His might at work on your inside. You have to be strong in it.

> *That he would grant you, according to the riches of his glory, to be*
> *strengthened with might by his Spirit in the inner man;*
> EPHESIANS 3:16

God wants you to be strengthened with might in your inner man by the help of the Holy Spirit. There is a strength in your inner man, but you have to be strong in the grace of God. There is room for improvement. There is room to grow in the grace of God. Be strengthened with might to live an ever-winning life.

To settle you: Grace came to give you an all-around settlement. Settlement means to have rest from your struggles, to be able to relax in Jesus' finished work and enjoy what He has done for you. Rest is when you desist from your works and relax to enjoy the fruits of the finished work of Christ. Grace has taken care of your settlement.

> *Come unto me, all ye that labour and are heavy laden,*
> *and I will give you rest.*
> MATTHEW 11:28

When you come to Jesus, the author and finisher of our faith and the epitome of grace, what you receive is rest from your labour. He did not come to enrol you into a school of labour, but to enrol you into a school of rest. All you will ever need has been paid for. There is no tuition fee, all fees have been paid. Your faith is what you need to change your level in this school of rest. The more you study the Word of His Grace and mix faith with it, more you change levels. There is no end to your lifting when you rest by faith in His finished work on the cross. Stop the struggles and rest in the finished work of God's grace. He said, "Come unto me, all you that labour," (in other words, all you that are striving in the flesh to fulfil the demands of the law to get blessed, struggling with habits, sin and all oppressions of the devil) "and are heavy laden," (are weary, weak and unfruitful) "and I will give you rest" (I will settle you, I will make you stop your struggles and let you enjoy the fruits of my finished work). This does not mean that you don't have to work or you don't have to live a righteous and holy life. No, it means that everything you will ever need in this life to work and make the most of it has been released already. It means that you have been made the righteousness of God in Christ and you are truly holy now. You don't have to do things to gain God's attention or acceptance. You already have His attention, you are accepted already. You are blessed already. You are loved already. What you would have done to get God to give you things, Jesus has already done. You are no longer struggling; you are enjoying. Grace came to settle you. His grace will surely settle whatever area of your life that needs settlement in Jesus name.

> *Saying with a loud voice, Worthy is the Lamb that was slain to receive power, and riches, and wisdom, and strength, and honour, and glory, and blessing.*
> REVELATION 5:12

These are the things He has received for you to ensure you are supernaturally settled. He has given you power, riches, wisdom, strength, honour, glory and blessing. All these were given to you by grace. You are not working for them. You are relying on and resting in Jesus' finished work by faith. He has brought you all these; you have to explore them for profitable living. It's not what He is going to do. It's what He has done for you. He was slain to receive everything for you to enjoy.

HOW TO BE STRONG IN GRACE

THE WORD

Your Word level determines your strength level. The more distant you are from the Word of God (which is a grace bank), the weaker you become in the battles of life. Go for the Word. Increase your hunger for the Word. Create a hunger for the Word of God's grace out of your relationship with Him. Leave religion and go for an intimate relationship with God. Be strong in your knowledge of the grace of God. Your depth of knowledge in grace determines the strength in your life. This ultimately determines your victorious living. It takes spiritual strength to be a victor. You don't lose any battle when you carry grace, it's your strength for winning. This is how you can increase your power content against the circumstances of life. Paul said to be strong in the grace that is in Christ Jesus.

> *If thou faint in the day of adversity, thy strength is small.*
> PROVERBS 24:10

If you faint when you are faced with challenges, your strength is small. Go for more strength; you can't afford to be stranded without strength. Increase your Word level to increase your strength level.

> *And now, brethren, I commend you to God, and to the word of his grace, which is able to build you up, and to give you an inheritance among all them which are sanctified.*
> ACTS 20:32

Grace builds in you the capacity needed to overcome life's challenges. The Word of God's grace is meant to strengthen you. It build's in you the inner strength to fight every battle. Grace is released from the Word of God as you study. You need faith to maximise grace, both of them work *Pari passu* (side by side with equal footing). You can't say you have faith without a knowledge of God's grace. It is your depth of grace that determines the level of your faith. You only have faith because you are exposed to what Christ has done for you. Faith comes by hearing and hearing by the Word of God (Romans 10:17). Your faith is hinged on the knowledge of the Word of Grace. As you know what has been done and what is available by grace, your faith is boosted up and the strength of your faith determines how well your life will turn out to be. There is no great faith without great grace and vice versa. Study and meditate on the Word of God's grace to be strong in the grace of God.

PRAYER OF REQUEST FOR MORE GRACE

Let us therefore come boldly unto the throne of grace, that we may obtain mercy, and find grace to help in time of need.
HEBREWS 4:16

Go for more strength when you are in need. When you don't know what to do, go to God in prayer to request more grace. Grace is always available.

He giveth power to the faint; and to them that have no might he increaseth strength.
ISAIAH 40:29

Whenever you ask for grace, your strength is increased. When you tired and you are fainting, go for grace. God gives fresh power. When you are unable to go on again, fresh strength is released. When you are failing and falling in your human strength, turn to His supernatural strength. When you come to the end of yourself, that's when you arrive at the beginning of God who is waiting to empower you. He wants you to request more grace. There is grace for everything. You have been limiting grace for a long time. It's time to see what it is and ask for more of it to maximise your destiny.

FASTING

> *But they that wait upon the Lord shall renew their strength; they shall mount up with wings as eagles; they shall run, and not be weary; and they shall walk, and not faint.*
> ISAIAH 40:31

When you are weak and fainting in your human strength, turn to fasting for strength renewal. There are spiritual battles, and there are physical battles. You don't engage in spiritual battles in the energy of the flesh. When you are faced with seemingly insurmountable mountains, you fast to expand your spiritual capacity to tackle them. Those habits, addictions, and various sins are not just bad choices you make; they are demonic influences arrayed against your destiny to paralyse you on earth so that you do not attain God's best for your life. You have been given the grace to be victorious, and you can wax strong in this grace when you fast. Grace is for you to stand strong through faith, not to keep falling. We are on a battlefield and grace is your strength. Your strength is renewable. You have what it takes to be at your best. Don't settle for anything the devil is throwing at you. You have been made victorious, start enforcing your victory by faith and engaging in whatever increases your spiritual strength, including fasting.

> *By Silvanus, a faithful brother unto you, as I suppose, I have written briefly, exhorting, and testifying that this is the* ***true grace of God wherein ye stand.***
> I PETER 5:12

True grace makes you stand. Be strong in the grace that you have received. It's your responsibility to see where you are now and where God expects you to be if you find out that you have not yet arrived. Engage in whatever it takes to shake off everything that is trying to limit you. Grace is not just a prayer you say at the end of a service or at a meal; it's a life you must live. Give expression to the power of the grace of God at work in you. Christ has done a finished work on your behalf; the devil is against what He has done for you. You have to fight back. Don't keep quiet. Take responsibility for the outcome of your life.

TAKE AWAY DECLARATIONS

I wax strong in my spirit; I'm filled with wisdom, and the grace of God is upon me (Luke 2:40)

I am strengthened with might in my inner man by the power of the Holy Ghost (Ephesians 3:16)

Father, your grace is sufficient for me, and your strength is made perfect in my weakness (II Corinthians 12:9)

I am made perfect, established, strengthened and settled by your grace in Jesus name (I Peter 5:10)

ABOUT THE AUTHOR

Sam Uhunoma was born and bred in Nigeria, lives in the United Kingdom, and studied Animal and Environmental Biology (Zoology) from *Delta State University - Abraka*. A committed member of his local church, he once held a position as the Vice President of *Royal World Campus Fellowship*, an arm of *Ever-Increasing Word of Life Ministries*. Sam was home cell leader at *Winners' Chapel - Abakaliki* during his National Youth Service Corps. He is currently an alter minister and a cell minister at *Winners' Chapel International - Manchester*. He is a lover of God and a product of grace.

Sam has proven with his achievements and life experiences that absolute dependency on God's grace through faith is the secret of all-around success. Today he is spreading his message of faith in God's grace to the world. He says all his achievements are traceable to God's grace at work, and he encourages others to shift focus from self to God.

ABOUT THE BOOK

LIVING A GRACE-CENTRED LIFE

In this book, you will discover:
How to find grace
How to mix faith with the Word of Grace
How to renew your mind with the Word of Grace
The unmerited favour dimension of grace
The love dimension of grace
How you can reign and rule in life by an abundance of grace
How to be strong in grace and more!

Living a grace-centred life is a powerful book designed to open you up to what grace has done for you and how you can practically live a grace life on earth. Grace message should not only excite you but incite you to take responsibility by faith to align with all God has destined you to be. Without grace, you cannot be all God has called you to be or do what God has called you to do. Grace is more than just a concept; it's a power. It's the power of God at work in you. It is God's ability at work in you when you have no ability. Grace is an expression of God's great love towards us. It is an expression of God's goodness towards undeserving people. You can't afford to settle for less when all things have been done for you by grace. All you need to enjoy a life of profit is to respond by faith in His finished work. Your faith is your now reality in the finished work of Christ.

Living
A Grace-Centred LIFE

EMAIL
samuhunoma@hotmail.com

FACEBOOK
SAM UHUNOMA

TWITTER
SAM UHUNOMA

INSTAGRAM
SAMIST1

OTHER BOOK

AVAILABLE AT:
Amazon and other fine bookstores and online venues.

Note from the Publisher

Are you a first time author?

Not sure how to proceed to get your book published?
Want to keep all your rights and all your royalties?
Want it to look as good as a Top 10 publisher?
Need help with editing, layout, cover design?
Want it out there selling in 90 days or less?

Visit our website for some exciting new options!

www.chalfant-eckert-publishing.com

www.ingramcontent.com/pod-product-compliance
Lightning Source LLC
LaVergne TN
LVHW051603070426
835507LV00021B/2738